Until Death Do Us Part: Stemming the Tide of Divorce in the Church

Additional books by Author

The Unseen Civil War: The Battle Between Our Flesh
and the Spirit (2014)

Until Death Do Us Part: Stemming the Tide of Divorce in the Church

Warren E Anderson

ISBN: 0996808108
ISBN 13: 9780996808101

Published in 2015 by Create Space, a DBA of On-Demand Publishing, LLC
7290 B Investment Drive
North Charleston, SC 29418

Acknowledgements

As I complete this book, I look back with thankfulness to some wonderful people who have been so instrumental in the completion of this book. For some of them, they have had such an awesome spiritual impact on my life, and the words that have come forth in this book.

Even though they are now with the Lord, I first want to acknowledge and thank my parents, Joseph and Hilda Anderson, for raising me to know, love and honor God. They lived godly lives both at church and at home and I was never confused about their salvation. They modeled a godly marriage before my siblings and me. I never once heard them argue, say a cross word to each other or disrespect each other in any way. I'm grateful for their example of marriage, which was part of the legacy of holiness they left my siblings and me. As I look back over their lives, I now understand that they saw their marriage as a part of their worship to God…and they lived it.

I'd also like to acknowledge and thank my pastor and spiritual father, Bishop Kenneth E. Moore, Sr., because he stirred me to truly and deeply search out the truths of God's Word. In his words, "shake every leaf of the tree to get everything God's Word is saying to us." Like Paul did for Timothy, Bishop Moore stirred in me the gift that God had already placed in me. And now, I can say like David, "Oh how I love your law! It is my meditation all the day." Pastor (Bishop) Moore, you know I love you and words can't express how grateful I am that God used you to stir His gift in me.

I also acknowledge the inspiration of our six children: Warren, Jr., Clayton, Andrea, Roberta, Donald and Gabrielle, who are not even aware of how they influenced and inspired me in writing this book. The truth is that they each gave me reasons to showcase a godly marriage before them. I especially want Andrea, Roberta and Gabrielle to know what a godly husband looks like so that when they look for husbands, they will remember the example that I am living before them as a godly husband to my wife...their mom and stepmom. For Warren, Jr., Clayton and Donald, my prayer is that they will see me fulfilling God's commands to me as the husband to their mom and stepmom...I want to be a living epistle for God in every way and especially in our marriage that in many ways is what our children see most. Guys, I love you all!

I also must acknowledge my brothers in Christ who are in my inner circle...you know who you are. They are the ones with whom I discussed the contents of this book as I was writing it and from whom I received such encouragement and prayers as I invested time and energy into completing this book. They unknowingly were my Aaron and Hur, holding up my arms, as I worked to keep the banner of God held up high in my walk with Him. Walking this Christian journey is so much easier and sweeter when you walk it with others who you know are striving to honor God with their lives just as you are...and with those you know who love you just as you love them...with no pretense.

I could go no further without acknowledging my wife Itzel who is my queen, my best friend, my girlfriend, my traveling companion, God's second best Gift to me. She is the woman whom I am convinced God designed specifically for me, and the one whom I love so much. Unlike Adam who threw his wife Eve under the bus when God confronted him about his sin, I want to truly thank God for this "woman You gave me." She is truly a Proverbs 31 wife! With each passing day, she compels me to love her even more because she immediately and continually responds in kind to my love for her. My wife is indeed a priceless gift from my God! This book would not be possible without her constant support, her untiring encouragement, and without her continual prayers for me. My wife...

my love...I am glad to be walking this life's journey with you by my side. Baby I love you!!!

Finally and most of all, I am indebted and grateful to my Lord and my Savior Jesus because without Him this book would not be possible! He loved me so much that for Him, I was to die for! He forgave all of my sins and amazingly He continues to use me in ways I couldn't even have imagined. His love covered my multitude of sins! What can I say; God is love. It is who He is, and it is His character. So this book is really about me living out God's character in my relationship with my wife...for that, I'm eternally grateful to my Lord and Savior Jesus Christ to whom belong all glory, majesty, dominion and power...forever! Because God placed this book in my spirit, my prayer is that this book will help all of us to become the husbands and wives He has purposed and commanded us to be...all to the glory of God!

Epigraph

*One of the good things that come of a true marriage is, that
there is one face on which changes come without your seeing
them; or rather there is one face which you can still see the same,
through all the shadows which years have gathered upon it.*

— GEORGE MACDONALD

Table of Contents

Introduction

THIS BOOK HAS BEEN YEARS in the making, although I didn't know this until about a year ago. It came out of the tragedy of my divorce, which I didn't want but it happened anyway. After it was all over...torn asunder by a judge who didn't know me from Adam...I remember sitting down one day and I had a conversation with God. As I sat there in the aftermath of that tragedy, I said these words, "God I need you. My plan apparently doesn't work." It was then that I heard God speaking into my heart. He said, "If you're ready, then it's time for you to really look at My plan for marriage...go to Ephesians 5:21-33 and there you will see the plan that I instituted for marriage."

Some reading this book may find that hard to believe...but if you are a believer and you don't hear God speaking into your heart, you should check your connection to God! I am absolutely, positively certain that God spoke into my heart about His plan for marriage. All you need to do now is ask the almost 3000 people at my church who see my wife and me Sunday in and Sunday out...or the numerous couples we have taught in pre-marriage classes or the married couples we have counseled...or our children...and they will tell you that I am for real and passionate about truly living out God's plan for marriage every day! I found out that God's plan, followed with all of your heart...can stand against anything that comes our way because He made marriage to be a permanent affair until death do us part!

But here's the rest of the story. Marriage today has taken on such a different intent than what God ordained or purposed from the beginning. Married couples now include heterosexual couples who have lived together for enough years that some states recognize them as "common-law" marriages. Married couples now also include same-sex couples that have garnered even main-stream support among previously *anti-gay marriage* politicians and common citizens alike, and now even among church denominations that previously stood against same-sex marriage.

However, let me take this moment to emphasize that this book is not about gay-bashing or anti-gay marriage. I am a born-again believer through and through, and although I don't accept nor agree with same-sex marriages or relationships in any shape form or fashion because God Himself called it an abomination, I love our gay citizens the same as God does. Furthermore, neither do I accept or agree with heterosexual pre-marital cohabitation.

This book first and foremost, is written to believers…those who have a personal relationship with God through Jesus Christ our Lord and Savior who is "the way, the truth, and the life," and the only way to God. Secondly, this book is written to those in the aforementioned group who are married, engaged or considering marriage. Please make no mistake, if you are not a born-again Christian, who strives daily to worship God in spirit and in truth, then most of this book will make no sense to you…and it will probably even offend you! If it does, I can't and nor will I apologize for propagating God's truth about marriage. But I hope that you will read this book and be challenged and convicted by God's Word!

Since I have jumped all the way into these waters that seem to stir such controversy these days, let me also add this one note. If you are not a born-again Christian who is striving daily to worship God in spirit and in truth, then getting married in a sacred house of God, such as a church, does nothing to guarantee God's blessings and the longevity of your marriage, any more than just going to church makes you a Christian on your way to heaven. On the other hand, if you are a born-again Christian who is striving daily to worship God in spirit and in truth, then you can even get married in a beautiful beach setting and God's blessings will follow you as you adhere to His plan for marriage.

The purpose of this book is to address an epidemic that has taken hold in the Church, which is the crippling, cancerous tide of divorce. It is time for us as believers to stem the tide of divorce in the Church! This epidemic has struck the church from the pulpit to the door...from pastors to ushers. Divorce in the Church has spread like a biological weapon of mass destruction and it has left broken ex-spouses, distraught and despondent children, crippled families in its wake and divided churches in its wake!

The surge of this typhoon-like epidemic has become so prevalent that we, as believing brothers and sisters in the family of God, no longer take note or feel sickened when Satan takes out another married couple in the Church. It's almost like we have given up on God's plan for marriage and see divorces in the Church as inevitable! The devil is a liar! The bottom-line purpose of this book is to help us, the Church, stem the tide of divorce in the Church!

Let's look at three short definitions of **"Stem the tide"** – According to the *American Heritage® Dictionary of Idioms* (2003) by Christine Ammer, "stem the tide" means to *"stop the course of a trend or tendency."* According to the *Cambridge Idioms Dictionary, 2nd ed.* (2006), "stem the tide" means to *"to stop something bad which is happening a lot."* Finally, according to the *Cambridge Dictionary of American Idioms* (2003), "stem the tide" means to *"stop something from increasing."* From these definitions, we can clearly see that divorce in the Church is a tide that must be turned. It's God's mandate for His Church!

How do we get there...to that point where we can stem the tide of divorce in the Church? In this book, we embark on a comprehensive examination of God's plan, and inherently, His intent for marriage. Our sole source for God's plan is from His Word and we will primarily examine God's plan for marriage as outlined in Ephesians 5:21-33, God's inspired words to the Apostle Paul. In addition, we also look at God's plan in the inspired words of the Apostle Peter and other Biblical authors.

By the time we reach the end of this book, we will have a solid grasp of God's plan for marriage. We will know for certain that it is God's intent and purpose for marriage to be a permanent union between a husband (a man) and his wife (a woman) and we will know that all other forms and formats of the world's accepted "marriages" are not of God, regardless of what the U.S Supreme Court or any other court or government says. Lastly, we will know what it takes for us, as believers chosen and called by God, to stem the tide of divorce in the Church…the body and bride of Christ! Are you ready? Let's get started!

Part One
God's Plan for Marriage

God created marriage. No government subcommittee
envisioned it. No social organization developed it. Marriage
was conceived and born in the mind of God.

—MAX LUCADO

WHEN I STARTED HIGH SCHOOL, I took a class on architectural drawing. What most impressed me about architectural drawing was that I was making a plan for designing a structure. If we look around us, especially in large urban areas such as Chicago, New York, Dallas, Miami, Seattle, Los Angeles or San Francisco, we will see architectural wonders. Many of these architectural wonders are skyscrapers dozens of floors high and some which span a city block or two. They are the result of the plans of the architect who designed these structures. What we see in these amazing structures are builders following the architect's plans to the tee...down to the last bolt without any deviations.

In Part One of this book, we will thoroughly examine God's plan for marriage. After all, He is the Great Architect of biblical or holy marriage. He designed the plan...His plan...the one that first and foremost brings glory and honor to Him...but which He also designed to benefit mankind, His creation. We will look at how and why God designed marriage between a man and a woman to be husband and wife, and to last a lifetime.

And like an architect who sadly watches his beloved building get demolished by a wrecking ball, God is also saddened and disappointed when a marriage He designed is demolished by divorce.

Therefore, we will look deeply into God's plan for marriage so that we, the Church, can stem the tide of divorce in God's family! I hope that as we thoroughly examine God's plan for marriage, you will highlight and underline areas, re-read various portions and write notes in this book as we commit to understand, internalize and live out God's plan for marriage in our own marriages. Are you ready…here we go!

CHAPTER 1

Marriage From the Beginning

*Take wives and have sons and daughters; take wives for your
sons, and give your daughters in marriage, that they may bear
sons and daughters; multiply there, and do not decrease.*

—JEREMIAH 29:6

THE FIRST AND THUS OLDEST of God's institutions is marriage. What is
marriage...what is its foundation...what is its structure? Webster defines
marriage as, *"The act of marrying, or the state of being married; legal union
of a man and a woman for life, as husband and wife; wedlock; matrimony."*
(Webster's Revised Unabridged Dictionary)

I particularly like this definition because it includes the structure of
marriage as God intended, "the union of a man and a woman for life, as
husband and wife!" This is the definition that this book emphasizes as the
one designed and ordered by God, regardless of what others propagate as
alternate structures for marriage. What's really important for those of us
reading this book is that we understand God's establishment of marriage
and subsequently, the establishment of the family.

From the very beginning, when God created the heavens and the
earth, and all living creatures including man, we can be absolutely sure
that God intended for there to be marriage between a man and a woman.

This marriage, the unbreakable union between a husband and his wife, was to fulfill God's purpose. Here it is from Genesis 1:26-28 (ESV):

> [26] Then God said, "Let us make man in our image, after our likeness. And let them have dominion over the fish of the sea and over the birds of the heavens and over the livestock and over all the earth and over every creeping thing that creeps on the earth." [27] So God created man in his own image, in the image of God he created him; male and female he created them. And God blessed them. [28] And God said to them, "Be fruitful and multiply and fill the earth and subdue it, and have dominion over the fish of the sea and over the birds of the heavens and over every living thing that moves on the earth.

Even though God had created other creatures, male and female animals, and Adam had named them, God knew that Adam would be lonely. The reason was that none of the other creatures were suitable for Adam as a companion. Therefore, God implemented his plan for marriage in Genesis 2:18 (ESV) when God said, *"It is not good that man should be alone; I will make him a helper fit for him."*

I laughed to myself as I thought of the numerous bumper stickers and T-shirts that contained verbiage degrading to wives such as "you can have my wife as long as I can keep my dog" or "wife for sale, take over the payments" or "I'll swap you my wife for a good horse." Yes, there have been a lot of jokes about replacing "a wife" with some other creature. Not to leave anyone out, likewise there have been numerous bumper stickers and T-shirts that contained verbiage degrading husbands. But in the end, none of those jokes are anything more than hollow ramblings and the words of people who do not understand God's plan for marriage. God said it isn't good for man to be alone; He never said it would be easy!

When we examine God's process of creation, we must take special note of how God's creation of man was different from the rest of His work in creation. God spoke the other creatures into existence; but He formed Adam *"of the dust of the ground, and breathed into his nostrils the breath of life; and man became a living soul.*" (Genesis 2:7 KJV) Likewise, God's creation of the woman and His implementation of marriage, between a man and a woman, was a very specific and detailed process found in Genesis 2:20-25 (KJV):

> 20 And Adam gave names to all cattle, and to the fowl of the air, and to every beast of the field; but for Adam there was not found an help meet for him. 21 And the LORD God caused a deep sleep to fall upon Adam, and he slept: and he took one of his ribs, and closed up the flesh instead thereof; 22 And the rib, which the LORD God had taken from man, made he a woman, and brought her unto the man. 23 And Adam said, This is now bone of my bones, and flesh of my flesh: she shall be called Woman, because she was taken out of Man. 24 Therefore shall a man leave his father and his mother, and shall cleave unto his wife: and they shall be one flesh. 25 And they were both naked, the man and his wife, and were not ashamed.

Let's take a quick moment to unpack God's creation of woman and implementation of marriage. The first thing we see is that after Adam had named all God's other creatures, it was very clear that there was no companion for him. Adam was different from all of the other creatures and therefore none of them could reason with or comfort him. I can imagine that although he was surrounded by a large gathering of animals, he still felt all alone. The second thing we can see is that God initiated His plan to do something about Adam's loneliness. Did you note that Adam didn't say something to God like, "God, there's no one that looks like me; where is my companion?" The all-knowing Creator already had a plan to remedy Adam's loneliness!

For this we can look at two scriptures in Genesis that explicitly address this problem for Adam. The first scripture, found in Genesis 1:27-28 (KJV), tells us:

> 27 So God created man in His own image, in the image of God created he him; male and female created he them. 28 And God

blessed them, and God said unto them, Be fruitful and multiply, and replenish the earth...

Let's look at one particular part of this scripture which is being attacked by many parts of our society today. Verse 27 tells us that God created man, Adam and Eve, as a male and a female. However, there are those in our societies who practice a homosexual lifestyle that claim they were born a different gender than their outward appearance. Some claim to be "a woman trapped in a man's body" or "a man trapped in a woman's body." They resort to transgender appearances or living as a transsexual. Some go as far as to have a doctor, a learned man yes...but a man no less, change their God created gender *to* the gender they ascribe to be. And they live a lifestyle that they want to live, even though it violates God's law.

The Bible tells us in Romans 1 that there are serious consequences for their lifestyle choices. I like the way the Eugene Peterson paraphrases it in Romans 1:26-28 (MSG):

> [26] Worse followed. Refusing to know God, they soon didn't know how to be human either—women didn't know how to be women, men didn't know how to be men. [27] Sexually confused, they abused and defiled one another, women with women, men with men—all lust, no love. And then they paid for it, oh, how they paid for it—emptied of God and love, godless and loveless wretches. [28] Since they didn't bother to acknowledge God, God quit bothering them and let them run loose.

The second scripture that explicitly address the issue of Adam not having a suitable mate is found in Genesis 2:21-24 (KJV):

> [21] And the Lord God caused a deep sleep to fall upon Adam, and he slept: and He took one of his ribs, and closed up the flesh instead thereof; [22] And the rib, which the Lord God had taken from man,

made He a woman, and brought her unto the man. ²³ And Adam said, This is now bone of my bones, and flesh of my flesh: she shall be called Woman, because she was taken out of man. ²⁴ Therefore shall a man leave his father and mother, and shall cleave unto his wife: and they shall be one flesh.

Verse 24 tells us something absolutely critical for biblical marriage, and believers must understand and internalize these three facts as the *laws* of biblical marriage.

The first *law* of biblical marriage is that the man [the husband] must leave his father and mother. Here, the Hebrew word for leave carries the connotation of "commit oneself to" or "forsake." Therefore, the husband forsakes his mother and father and commits himself to his wife. Now, this forsaking does not mean the husband turns his back on his parents; rather, it means that he forsakes them in terms of moving to a different habitation to live with his wife. In other words, he sets up a different household. Even in the bible times when families lived in tents and a son married but remained as a part of the nomadic tribe, after a son married, he and his wife moved into their own tent. That meant that the son was establishing his own household, which was distinctly separate from his father and mother's household.

The second *law* of biblical marriage is that the man [the husband] must cleave unto his wife. The Hebrew meaning for cleave is to "cling, stick, or be joined together." This certainly points to the fact that God intends for marriage to be a permanent joining or union between a husband and wife. In fact, Jesus straightened the Pharisee out on this same subject in Matthew 19:3-6 (ESV):

> ³ And Pharisees came up to him and tested him by asking, "Is it lawful to divorce one's wife for any cause?" ⁴ He answered, "Have you not read that he who created them from the beginning made them male and female, ⁵ and said, 'Therefore a man shall leave his father and his mother and hold fast to his wife, and

the two shall become one flesh'? ⁶ So they are no longer two but one flesh. What therefore God has joined together, let not man separate.

As I contemplated this cleaving or joining together, the Holy Spirit gave me an analogy that really resonated in my mind. When I was in high school, I had a welding shop class. I recall that we were given two pieces of metal and we had to connect them together by welding them. What I learned is that in order to make a true, lasting connection, one must first understand the process. I learned that I needed to place the two pieces of metal together so they were touching at the point where they would be connected. I then used a gas torch and a welding rod to heat the two pieces of metal until they became molten at the connection point. The two pieces of metal become welded or truly connected when the molten points are fused together with the now molten welding rod.

In biblical marriage, the Father is the welder and the Holy Spirit is the welding rod. The Father puts a husband and wife together and the Holy Spirit does His job of fusing them together. A proper weld is inseparable and so is a biblically joined marriage. Let me add one last thing about the husband cleaving to his wife. In order for this to happen, the husband and wife must be in a biblically-based, monogamous marriage. Any other marriage make-up is unbiblical!

The third *law* of biblical marriage is that the husband and wife "shall" be one flesh. The Hebrew word for *shall be* means "to be, become, come to pass." According to the Vines Old Testament Dictionary, the word *be* "*makes a strong statement about the being or presence of a person or thing.*" This means that when the first two laws of biblical marriage happen, then the third law will absolutely happen...it will be so! This becoming one flesh is the fulfillment of my welding analogy above. This isn't something that takes a theologian to interpret for us; it is very simple. God intended the union between a husband and wife to be inseparable...period!

In Matthew 19:7-9 (ESV), Jesus continued his discussion with the Pharisees regarding divorce:

[7] They said to him, "Why then did Moses command one to give a certificate of divorce and to send her away?" [8] He said to them, "Because of your hardness of heart Moses allowed you to divorce your wives, but from the beginning it was not so. [9] And I say to you: whoever divorces his wife, except for sexual immorality, and marries another, commits adultery.

This a great place to comment on a growing trend in divorces, especially in the Church where marital infidelity may not have been the issue. Over and over couples are using the excuse of "irreconcilable differences" as the reason for their divorce. It's sad to say, but this is perhaps the biggest excuse used by those in the Church! We hear things like, "We just couldn't work it out...we couldn't communicate!" Therefore, "irreconcilable differences" has become the culprit that leads to and justifies divorces in the Church!

In the scripture above, both the Pharisees and Jesus were referring to Deuteronomy 24:1 – *"When a man hath taken a wife, and married her, and it come to pass that she find no favour in his eyes, because he hath found some uncleanness in her: then let him write her a bill of divorcement, and give it in her hand, and send her out of his house."* The Pharisees of course tried to trick Jesus by asking Him why Moses commanded a husband to give his wife a bill of divorce when she no longer pleased him. But Jesus countered their words with the truth that Moses did not command divorce; rather Moses suffered or allowed the Jews to divorce because of the hardness of their hearts. In other words, Moses allowed the Israelite husbands to divorce their wives as a last resort, if the husband found some uncleanness in her.

It's important to note that this uncleanness was not an issue of sexual immorality, such as adultery, since that would have been punishable by death (Genesis 22:22-23). Rather, this uncleanness referred to some violation of the Mosaic laws of purity. For example, if a Jewish husband had sex with his wife, but she neglected to tell him that her menstrual cycle had started, this would be an issue of uncleanness or impurity for him. In fact, according to Jewish Law (Halakha) from the Code of Maimonides

(Mishneh Torah), "*It is specifically forbidden for a man to have sexual intercourse with a menstruating woman. Any man who lies with such a woman so that her blood is on him is impure for seven days, and any bed that he then lies on is impure; both of them will be cut off from their people.*"

I can only imagine that in a situation like the one I just mentioned, a husband who wanted to seem particularly pious would perhaps take this opportunity to rid himself of a wife he no longer wanted, under the guise that she had made him impure...even if she didn't know her menstrual cycle had started. This wouldn't be a well-veiled scheme, especially since there was a ritual of ceremonial purification for situations like this. However, a Jewish husband could divorce his wife for this. But in Matthew 19:9 (ESV), Jesus was very clear when He told the Pharisees, "*And I say to you: whoever divorces his wife, except for sexual immorality, and marries another, commits adultery.*"

Jesus did something very specific and very significant, and He left no room for doubt. He established fornication or adultery (sexual immorality) as the only biblical allowable exceptions for divorce in which the offended spouse would not be guilty of adultery. This is the same exception Jesus spoke of concerning divorce in Matthew 5:32. But in both verses, Jesus does not command divorce, even when a spouse has been unfaithful! He permitted divorce so that when either party remarries, especially the innocent party, they would not carry the shame and guilt of being an adulterer.

As we have previously stated, God designed marriage to be between a man and a woman who become husband and wife until they are separated by death. God took a rib from Adam's side and made Eve. This indicates the woman has a clear connection with the man, and Adam's love response was immediate. Here's a thought! Adam and Eve were the first married couple. They truly became husband and wife before God who performed their wedding ceremony with His own words as their wedding vows! He told them to be fruitful and multiply and replenish the earth. As believers who want to obey God, we must see marriage as God sees it. We must understand God's purpose and design for marriage, and willingly commit ourselves to the permanence of biblical marriage.

Chapter One Questions to Ponder and Discuss

1. Do I believe it is God's plan for marriage to be "the union of a man and a woman *for life*, as husband and wife?" Or do I have a different belief?

   Yes!

2. Have I been a part of making jokes about replacing my spouse with someone else or something else? If so, have I really considered the how those jokes might be affecting my spouse?

   Yes. I feel sad and I repent.

3. What are my thoughts about the special way and care God took in making woman? As a husband, what should I do with this information? As a wife, what should I do with this information?

   A wife was a gift to Adam.
   He had to wait for it, probably
   so he would appreciate it.
   A part of him.

4. Do I believe and ascribe to God's format for marriage, that is, between a man and a woman? What are my thoughts about marriage unions between individuals of the same sex?

> Yes.
>
> Same sex marriage are not of God.

5. As a husband, which of my actions plainly demonstrate that I have truly left my father and mother and am cleaving to my wife? As a wife, why must I equally see the importance of leaving my parents and cleaving to my husband?

> My husband and I have created a new household, separate from my mother and father.

6. How have my spouse and I discussed how we will prevent divorce from ever becoming an option or even a topic of discussion for us? What preventive measures have we put into place?

> We have sought godly counseling when have reached an impasse.

CHAPTER 2

Pre-Marriage Behavior of Believers

Beloved, I urge you as sojourners and exiles to abstain from
passions of the flesh, which wage war against your soul.

— 1 Peter 2:11

BEFORE WE EXAMINE THE ROLES and responsibilities for the husband and wife, I feel compelled to take a little time and speak to how we as believers ought to behave as engaged or dating couples. The first thing we can be sure of is this: as believers, we are not to have a "trial run" where we are living like a married couple. That means we are not to cohabitate and/or engage in pre-marital sex. I know…everyone else is doing it! But, we are not everyone else; according to 1 Peter 2:9 (KJV), we are God's *"chosen generation, a royal priesthood, an holy nation."*

Let's look at some pre-marriage behavior from the Matthew 1:18-20 (KJV):

> ¹⁸ Now the birth of Jesus Christ was on this wise: When as his mother Mary was espoused to Joseph, before they came together, she was found with child of the Holy Ghost. ¹⁹ Then Joseph her husband, being a just man, and not willing to make her a pub- lick example, was minded to put her away privily. ²⁰ But while he thought on these things, behold, the angel of the Lord appeared

unto him in a dream, saying, Joseph, thou son of David, fear not to take unto thee Mary thy wife: for that which is conceived in her is of the Holy Ghost.

From Matthew 1:18, we read that "...Mary was espoused or betrothed to Joseph, before they came together..." In today's terms, that means that Mary and Joseph were engaged to be married. However, unlike a very great number of engaged couples today, they did not live together and nor had they engaged in pre-marital sex. We know this to be the case because Mary was impregnated by the Holy Ghost and when Joseph found out she was pregnant, he contemplated quietly divorcing her to save her from embarrassment.

One of the reasons I wanted to talk about pre-marriage behavior is because in our society, an engagement takes on another aspect that is different from the espousal or betrothal of the Bible times. The Holman Bible Dictionary provided a great explanation for betrothal:

Betrothal was the act of engagement for marriage in Bible times and was as binding as marriage. Old Testament: The biblical terms, betrothal and espousal, are almost synonymous with marriage, and as binding. Betrothal and marriage comprised a moral and spiritual principle for the home and society. The penalty under the Law of Moses for disrupting this principle by adultery, rape, fornication, or incest was death by stoning (Deuteronomy 22:23-30). Later under some circumstances the Jewish legal system allowed divorce. The forgiving love and grace of God for his adulterous people is demonstrated by Hosea buying back his adulterous wife and restoring her to his home and protection (Hosea 2:19-20). This means that forgiveness takes precedence over stoning or divorce.

New Testament: Mary and Joseph were betrothed but did not live together until their wedding. When Mary came to be with child during betrothal, Joseph decided to quietly divorce her. In a dream from God, the apparent unfaithfulness of Mary was explained to Joseph as a miracle of the Holy Spirit. This miracle gave emphasis to the unique human and divine nature of Jesus Christ. Paul used the betrothal concept to explain the ideal relationship that exists between the church as a chaste virgin being presented to Christ (2 Corinthians 11:2).

http://www.studylight.org/dic/hbd/view.cgi?n=906

So frequently today, when a person becomes engaged, their friends often push them, sometimes with little prodding needed, to "sow their wild oats" as much as they can before they "say I do." I've heard guys tell an engaged guy, "Man, you'd better sleep with all the women you can now because in two months, you're going to have to sleep with the same woman for the rest of your life." That kind of talk and behavior tells me two things. First, for many of today's couples, marriage is often seen as some obligation that will result in all of the fun of sexual intimacy going out the door...how wrong they are! The second thing it tells me is that even many unbelievers recognize that marriage between a husband and wife is supposed to be monogamous and forever.

Let me park on this point for just a moment. This is a great place for us to consider and embrace what the Bible tells us about listening to and hanging out with the wrong people. In Psalm 1:1-2 (ESV) we read *"Blessed is the man who walks not in the counsel of the wicked, nor stands in the way of sinners, nor sits in the seat of scoffers; but his delight is in the law of the LORD, and on his law he meditates day and night."*

The funny thing is that our ungodly counselors, whether they are family, friends or co-workers, think they are giving us good advice. However, as believers, we must choose to listen to the Holy Spirit from whom we receive godly wisdom. Look at these two scriptures. From Proverbs 1:10 (MSG), we read *"Dear friend, if bad companions tempt you, don't go along with them."* From Proverbs 2:10-13 (ESV), we read *"For wisdom will come into your heart, and knowledge will be pleasant to your soul; discretion will watch over you, understanding will guard you, delivering you from the way of evil, from men of perverted speech, who forsake the paths of uprightness to walk in the ways of darkness."* The bottom line is this; if anyone is telling us to do something that violates God's Word, we as believers must always choose to be obedient to the Holy Spirit and follow God's Word...end of story!

Okay, let's look at an Old Testament example of betrothal. Genesis 19:14 (ESV) shows us where a betrothal carried the force of marriage in the bible times: *"So Lot went out and said to his sons-in-law, who were to marry his daughters, "Up! Get out of this place, for the Lord is about to destroy the city." But he seemed to his sons-in-law to be jesting."* From this scripture, we can see that Lot saw his daughters' fiancés as his sons-in-laws, even thought they had not yet had the official wedding and his daughters had not moved into their husbands' homes.

Now, I know some of you will be quick to point out that Genesis 19:14 (KJV) seems to indicate that Lot's sons-in-laws had already married his daughters: *"And Lot went out, and spake unto his sons in law, which married his daughters, and said, Up, get you out of this place; for the LORD will destroy this city. But he seemed as one that mocked unto his sons in law."* I would probably have thought the same thing except if we go up a few verses and look in Genesis 19:8 (KJV), we read, *"Behold now, I have two daughters which have not known man; let me, I pray you, bring them out unto you, and do ye to them as is good in your eyes: only unto these men do nothing; for therefore came they under the shadow of my roof."* In this verse we see that Lot's daughters were still virgins because he said they have not known man. Therefore, Lot's daughters still lived in his house and had not gone through the marriage ceremony and thus had not consummated their marriages to their husbands.

Since this book is written especially to believers, I am compelled to talk about the pre-marriage behavior expected from believers. The bible certainly contains scriptures that address how unmarried, but courting believers and all unmarried believers for that matter ought to behave. Please understand; this is not suggested behavior! Rather, this is behavior that God commands and expects from unmarried believers. This behavior of sexual purity coincides with God's command for us to "live holy for He is holy" (1 Peter 1:16).

LESSONS FROM A SHUNAMMITE GIRL

The first thing we receive is a warning from the Song of Solomon. King Solomon's fiancée, the Shunammite, gives this warning: "*Oh, let me warn you, sisters in Jerusalem, by the gazelles, yes, by all the wild deer: Don't excite love, don't stir it up, until the time is ripe—and you're ready.*" We read this warning three times in Eugene Petersen's MSG Bible from Songs 2:7, 3:5, and 8:4. This warning is applicable to single male believers as well as to single female believers. The Shunammite realized that when she was around her beau, her body would betray her! The feelings of sensual love were strong and pulled at her. She fought hard to maintain her purity. If the Shunammite faced those feelings and struggles in her day, when both women and men dressed much, much more modestly than we do today, can you imagine the struggle single believers face today?

In the time of the Bible and even up to perhaps the late 19th or very early 20th century, couples and especially unmarried women, were always chaperoned when they went on dates while courting! There were no romantic dinners with low lights or slow dancing. At dances, to borrow a term from our Catholic brothers and sisters, the couple always kept "the Holy Spirit between them!"

In an online article by Michelle J. Hoppe, titled "Courting the Victorian Woman," Ms. Hoppe provided the following insight on the pre-marriage behavior of courting couples, especially for the woman:

Great care had to be taken at these public affairs, so as not to offend a possible suitor or his family. A single woman never walked out alone. Her chaperone had to be older and preferably married. If she had progressed to the stage of courtship in which she walked out with a gentleman, they always walked apart. A gentleman could offer his hand over rough spots, the only contact he was allowed with a woman who was not his fiancée.

Proper women never rode alone in a closed carriage with a man who wasn't a relative. She would never call upon an unmarried gentleman at his place of residence. She couldn't receive a man at home if she was alone. Another family member had to be present in the room. A gentlewoman never looked back after anyone in the street, or turned to stare at others at church, the opera, etc. No impure conversations were held in front of single women. No sexual contact was allowed before marriage. Innocence was demanded by men from girls in his class, and most especially from his future wife.

http://www.literary-liaisons.com/article009.html

Today, this type of pre-marriage behavior is seen as absurd and old fashioned. The vast majority of people in the world would suggest that this is downright prudish behavior...and perhaps they would be right. However, it does not change the fact that this seemingly prudish and absurd behavior went a long way in helping couples adhere to the Shunammite's warnings and to God's command for believers to "flee from fornication!" It certainly is a fact that during those times, there were not nearly as many marriages as there are today that occur or occur prior to the previously planned nuptials date, because the woman got pregnant out of wedlock. Today, pre-marriage pregnancies have almost become an acceptable norm.

We cannot be so naïve as to think that the couples who adhered to chaste behavior did not experience the pull of their passions toward each other. Nor can we even assume that just because they dressed modestly, certainly unlike many couples do today, that they were not affected by their sexual desires for each other. I believe we can strongly assume that regardless of what they wore or even the chaperones accompanying them, they were still affected by the physical and intimate emotional attraction they felt for each other.

The second thing we can see from the Song of Solomon is the importance of virginity. Notice, I did not specify the importance of the woman being a virgin, because it is equally as important for the man to be a virgin. We live in a society where for so long it was appropriate for a woman to maintain her sexual purity, but men were encouraged to sow their wild oats before getting married. We've all heard the stories of male friends taking their "virgin" male friend to a legal brothel in places like Nevada... perhaps a father thought he needed to take his son to such a place for his first sexual experience. But then, we as men have an attitude when a woman doesn't remain a virgin...we look at her like she is damaged goods, when in fact she's only done what most of us men have done...shouldn't the rules be the same...and isn't what's good for the goose also good for the gander...or do we as men think we're exempt from God's mandate to remain sexually pure?

We'll address this more later, but perhaps Jesus provided a clear answer to this question in the passage we find in John 8:3-11, where the Scribes brought a woman to Him who had been caught in the very act of adultery. They then proceeded to tell Jesus that the Law of Moses required that she be stoned. Jesus' response to them was simply, "he that is without sin cast the first stone." Jesus did not specify a sin, but His implication was apparently clear to those men because they all left without any of them throwing a single stone.

As we continue with the Shunammite, in Song of Solomon 8:8-12 (MSG), the Shunammite gives us an insight into how important it was for her to maintain her virginity and the steps taken to ensure her virginity:

My brothers used to worry about me: 'Our little sister has no breasts. What shall we do with our little sister when men come asking for her? She's a virgin and vulnerable, and we'll protect her. If they think she's a wall, we'll top it with barbed wire. If they think she's a door, we'll barricade it.' Dear brothers, I'm a walled-in virgin still, but my breasts are full— And when my lover sees me, he knows he'll soon be satisfied. King Solomon may have vast vineyards in lush, fertile country, Where he hires others to work the ground. People pay anything to get in on that bounty. But my vineyard is all mine, and I'm keeping it to myself. You can have your vast vineyards, Solomon, you and your greedy guests!

What if our youth, both girls and boys, saw virginity as something to be proud of instead of something to be ashamed of? What if the rushing waves of "get all the sex you can before marriage" and the era of "friends with benefits" that has become so rampant within our societies could be slowed or even stopped...and what if we entered a new era where our youth all across the world joined the True Love Waits (TLW) movement of teenagers and young adults who have pledged to God to abstain from pre-marital sex and save themselves for marriage? I found the following online regarding the TLW movement: The True Love Waits pledge states:

Believing that true love waits, I make a commitment to God, myself, my family, my friends, my future mate and my future children to be sexually abstinent from this day until the day I enter a biblical marriage relationship.

http://en.wikipedia.org/wiki/True_Love_Waits

In addition, the TLW movement promotes sexual purity, which encompasses not only abstaining from sexual intercourse before marriage, but also abstaining from sexual thoughts, sexual touching, pornography, and actions that are known to lead to sexual arousal. For sure, TLW is sending out the right message, and of course, they have their haters! But then again, there will always be those who criticize and hate the truth...Jesus had his haters and so will all who stand up for the truth of God's word.

You may be wondering about the benefits of remaining sexually pure until one enters a biblical marriage, as well as potential consequences of sexual promiscuity prior to marriage. Perhaps this true story will help. I once worked for several years with a guy named Steve. He was reserved, but I later found out he is a Christian. He didn't think he was better than anyone else or holier than anyone else; he was simply very careful about who he surrounded himself with. One of the things that blessed me about Steve was his testimony about him and his wife Pam. They met in high school and were high school sweethearts. But they both remained sexually pure until they were married. Pam is the only woman Steve has ever slept with and Steve is the only man Pam has ever slept with.

One of the things I realized from Steve's story is that he can't be plagued by memories of other sexual relationships. Satan has a way of bringing up the past, especially relationships that were unbiblical. When a couple experiences a rough patch, Satan will bring to mind previous romantic relationships...and that spells trouble for the couple who often fantasizes about the sex involved in those previous relationships. But for Steve and Pam, they only have their thoughts of each other...what a blessing that must be...to not have thoughts of past relationships plague your mind! So, I believe Steve and Pam would say that the benefit of remaining sexually pure for them was priceless! I recently learned that Steve had retired from a job he loved. He retired because his wife...his best friend... his sweetheart, had an early onset of Alzheimer's and Steve has become her primary caregiver. For me, Steve and Pam's marriage epitomizes the title of this book: "Until Death Do Us Part!"

One of the trends I have noticed lately, especially among those in church, is the increasing number of couples who are getting married with the bride already pregnant. Now, please don't misunderstand me; I am not judging them! I am simply saying that pre-marital pregnancy is one of the consequences of pre-marital sex. On the other hand, I can't help but think that a perhaps more than a few church-goers have made the decision to abort a fetus rather than endure the *perceived* potential problems or shame associated with an out-of-wedlock, unplanned/unwanted pregnancy.

However, this is not the answer. In addition, perhaps an even larger, but hidden consequence of pre-marital sex is the sexually transmitted diseases (STDs) that run rampant in our society. Unlike a pregnancy, many STDs can remain hidden to others while the exposed individual receives treatment. The government, schools, and planned-parenthood entities recommend safe-sex techniques, such as the use of condoms and dental dams for our youth to prevent pregnancies and STDs. However, this too is not the answer…it only perpetuates the ever increasing problems of pre-marital sex!

The answer for pre-marital behavior, especially among unmarried Christian believers, is found in the truths of God's word. I must say that I am really, really disappointed in the explosion of the new age thinking that it's okay for single believers to freely engage in pre-marital sex. I read an article in Ebony Magazine's May 2012 issue, titled *"Single, Saved, and Having Sex."* There was a bold statement underneath the article's title that said, "A majority of young Christians are foregoing abstinence, even as they keep the faith." A young woman, who stated she is a Christian, recounted her decision to have pre-marital sex. She said:

> My mind was telling me one thing, my body another. I was grown [and] longing to be touched. I am not perfect; I struggle with sin. I strive to live a righteous life. Just because I have a Bible on my nightstand and condoms in the drawer doesn't mean I love God any less or that He doesn't love me.
>
> *www.ebony.com/love-sex/single-saved-and-having-sex#ixzz2pCup4tKX*

This young woman is absolutely correct; God does still loves her! The issue of love is not God's problem—it is her problem! To be sure, this young woman's belief about sin in general, and particularly sexual sins, have grown prevalent throughout the Church. However, this young woman's *choice* to practice a life of pre-marital sex isn't a question of God's love for her. The real question is about the depth of her love for God. In John 14:15 (ESV), Jesus said *"If you love me, you will keep my commandments."*

Well, I've jumped in this water; I might as well go all the way. From this young woman's statement, it appears she loves herself more than she loves God. How can I say that you ask? It's because anytime we choose to satisfy our flesh over God's commands, then we have replaced God as the one sitting on the throne of our lives.

The other problem I believe that this young woman has is that she is simply displaying her Bible on her nightstand and the truths contained in the Bible are not being fed into her heart. In Psalm 119:105 (ESV), we read *"Your word is a lamp to my feet and a light to my path."* It's not enough just to have a deadbolt lock on your front door; you actually have to engage the lock in order to keep out burglars! Satan and our own fleshly desires is that burglar who is trying to break into our fellowship with God and steal our joy! This young woman having her Bible on her nightstand is a lot like many of us who have our Bibles in the back window area of our cars... people see it when they walk by...the sun hits it and the pages start to roll up and turn yellow like we've been reading it...but we simply just have the Bible on display.

Believe me; I'm not at all judging this young woman. However, I do stand on the truth of God's Word. In 2 Peter 1:3 (NKJV), we read that God *"According as his divine power hath given unto us all things that pertain unto life and godliness..."* In other words, as believers, we have the power of the Holy Spirit living inside of us and therefore, we are no longer slaves to sin...when we sin, it is not because we have to...it is because *we choose* to sin! Christ delivered us from the power of sin when He gave his life on the cross. We can see this very thing in Romans 6:15-18 (NLT):

> 15 Well then, since God's grace has set us free from the law, does that mean we can go on sinning? Of course not! 16 Don't you realize that you become the slave of whatever you choose to obey? You can be a slave to sin, which leads to death, or you can choose to obey God, which leads to righteous living. 17 Thank God! Once you were slaves of sin, but now you wholeheartedly obey this

teaching we have given you. [18] Now you are free from your slavery to sin, and you have become slaves to righteous living.

This young woman's thinking isn't new! It is a repeat of the same issue Paul addressed in many of his epistles and which John addressed in the book of 1 John. It is called *Gnosticism*. Gnostics believed in dualism. They saw the body as separate from the spirit. They only saw their connection with God as "through the spirit;" so therefore, they could do whatever they wanted to do with their body. In Romans 12:1-2 (ESV), Paul said, *"I appeal to you therefore, brothers, by the mercies of God, to present your bodies as a living sacrifice, holy and acceptable to God, which is your spiritual worship. Do not be conformed to this world, but be transformed by the renewal of your mind, that by testing you may discern what is the will of God, what is good and acceptable and perfect."*

When we consider God's mercy toward us, the very least we can do as believers is to give ourselves totally to Him, both body and spirit! Furthermore, in Galatians 5:13 (ESV), Paul warned us as believers that although we were called to freedom, we were *"not to use your freedom as an opportunity for the flesh..."* God's standard has never changed! In Leviticus 11:44 (ESV) and 1 Peter 1:16 (ESV), He said, *"Be ye holy for I am holy."* The Bible has plenty to say about sexual immorality, whether it's pre-marital sex or extra-marital sex... whether it's fornication or adultery! Consider these additional scriptures:

1 Corinthians 6:18 (ESV) - Flee from sexual immorality. Every other sin a person commits is outside the body, but the sexually immoral person sins against his own body.

1 Thessalonians 4:3-5 (ESV) - For this is the will of God, your sanctification: that you abstain from sexual immorality; that each one of you know how to control his own body in holiness and honor, not in the passion of lust like the Gentiles who do not know God.

Hebrews 13:4 (ESV) - Let marriage be held in honor among all, and let the marriage bed be undefiled, for God will judge the sexually immoral and adulterous.

Colossians 3:5 (ESV) – Put to death therefore what is earthly in you: sexual immorality, impurity, passion, evil desire, and covetousness, which is idolatry.

1 Thessalonians 4:3 (ESV) - For this is the will of God, your sanctification: that you abstain from sexual immorality.

Galatians 5:19 (ESV) - Now the works of the flesh are evident: sexual immorality, impurity, sensuality...

Ephesians 5:3 (ESV) - But sexual immorality and all impurity or covetousness must not even be named among you, as is proper among saints.

As believers, whether single or married, we must follow God's word. We can't allow the flesh to rule over us. Jesus set us free from the power or mastery of sin over our lives; so therefore, how can we continue to obey the flesh? In Romans 6:1 (KJV), Paul asked and answered this very question: *"What shall we say then? Shall we continue in sin, that grace may abound? God forbid. How shall we, that are dead to sin, live any longer therein? Know ye not, that so many of us as were baptized into Jesus Christ were baptized into his death?"*

I'm particularly fond of the way Romans 6:1 reads in the MSG Bible: *"So what do we do? Keep on sinning so God can keep on forgiving? I should hope not! If we've left the country where sin is sovereign, how can we still live in our old house there? Or didn't you realize we packed up and left there for good? That is what happened in baptism. When we went under the water, we left the old country of sin behind; when we came up out of the water, we entered into the new country of grace—a new life in a new land! That's what baptism into the life of Jesus means."*

So I want to encourage and strengthen our single believers...whether you are in a courtship leading to marriage, a dating relationship to better get to know a fellow believer or not in a relationship and you have chosen to honor God with your entire being. Let your worship be in spirit and in truth…in sincerity and in truth. In Daniel 1:8, Daniel purposed or resolved in his heart that he would not defile himself with the delicacies offered from the king's table. You must keep in mind that Satan is trying to offer you the delicacies of the flesh and he is bombarding your senses with his offerings. I exhort you to properly respond to God's grace as I mentioned in the previous paragraph.

I want to share with you a scripture from Titus 2:11-12 (KJV), which I have personally taken to heart and which drives my response to Satan's daily bombardment of sensual stimuli into our lives: *"For the grace of God that bringeth salvation hath appeared to all men, Teaching us that, denying ungodliness and worldly lusts, we should live soberly, righteously, and godly, in this present world."* These words compel me to daily strive to live holy; I hope they will have the same effect on you!

There is a blessing with choosing to honor God! There is a blessing in choosing to abstain from fornication. If you have chosen and succeeded in remaining a virgin, even in the pressures of this world to engage in pre-marital sex, then know that God will honor what you have done and committed to Him! If you are not a literal virgin, but you have come to know the Lord as your God and Savior, then you can still honor Him by choosing to live as a newly formed "spiritual virgin" who will say, "No sex until after I say I do to my spouse!" You can do it…whether you are still a virgin from your physical birth or a virgin since your spiritual birth… YOU CAN DO IT!

As I conclude this chapter, consider the stories below from two couples who chose sexual purity in order to honor God!

Nikki's Story

Twenty-four years, 1 month, and 29 days. Yes, I was a virgin for the first 24 years, 1 month, and 29 days of my life, until the day I married my husband. Ask me any day, any time and those numbers will flow out with ease, with no hesitation. Hopefully, that helps you to see that the fact of my waiting does not negate the truth that I longed for it, I wanted it. Yes, my desire to engage in sexual intercourse, though I'd never had it was very strong... maybe in part because of how people all around me hyped it up. I wanted to know what I was missing! Based on the hype happening without and the desires blazing within, I was missing out on something amazing and I wanted it! My desire for it was strong, but so was my love for God. I knew what He called for: abstaining from sexual immorality, fleeing fornication and I loved Him— God that is.

I had been graced in my journey to come across that all-important scripture, I John 5:3, "Loving God means keeping His commandments." I couldn't afford not to love God given the way He'd loved me. Nor was I content using that all too common, inexcusable cop-out, "God knows my heart." So I was willing to do what it took to position myself in such a way that I dare not fall prey to the desire within before proper time. I'd seen too many of my acquaintances do it—Christians, apparent God-lovers--fall prey to that blazing desire within before time. I did not want to fall prey.

My flesh wanted sex, my spirit wanted to please God, to keep His commandments, to love Him. So what was I to do? Somewhere along my journey I was graced to learn that my entire walk with Christ is a battle between my flesh and my spirit and ultimately what it boils down to is whichever one is stronger is the one that wins. Whichever one I feed is the one that grows stronger. As I reflect back on the grace God gave me to abstain, and I compare my story to others who had set out with the same intentions I had, but didn't see it through, the difference maker was that I "starved" my flesh and fed my spirit. How did I starve my flesh? Well, I was very selective about the music I listened to. If the lyrics didn't promote the path I desired to be on then I couldn't allow it to feed me. If the music was talking about "booty calls" and bumping and grinding, and touching and gyrating I refused to allow it into my spirit. Even now I can hear my dad saying over the pulpit, "You ain't married! What are you doing listening to that?!" In starving my flesh I also refused to indulge in conversations of a sexual nature. That is not to say that I didn't have them in an appropriate context—but to allow my mind to go and explore where I had decided I did not want my body to be was a restriction I placed on myself.

How did I feed my spirit? Well, it started with a daily QUIT—quiet, uninterrupted, intimate time—with God. This time included reading His Word, this time included prayer, and it included meditation that I took with me throughout the day. I also fed my spirit by committing verses to memory. I had scriptures on the walls of my dorm room, on the screensaver of my computer, posted in my car, etc. I fed my spirit by being mindful of the company I kept. Just like with music, if the people didn't promote the path I desired to be on, then I could not keep company with them. I recalled that 1 Corinthians 15:33 said, "Bad company corrupts good character." In being mindful of these things and being careful about what I nourished, my flesh grew and remained weak in comparison to the robust strength of my spirit.

However, with this robust strength of spirit, I would be an unmarried virgin today if it had not been for the man I chose to be in relationship with, grow with, and marry. It'd be negligence on my part in giving this account if I did not speak on the importance of dating someone who's love for God and plans for showing that love is the same as yours. When I met my husband, he too was a virgin and had every intention of being one until he married. We grew together. We did memory verses, prayed together, read books together, went to bible study together, fed our spirits together, abstained from sex together. So here we are now, after 2-1/2 years of dating, 8 years of marriage and a 4-year-old son, happy, loving each other, having only known one another and well-pleased. We can't help but wonder if much of the beauty and blessing we experience in our life together is a result of having honored God's commandment to "flee fornication." We are inclined to believe so. Let it be known that not everybody "is doing it!" Trust God's way; trust His plan for your life. He makes it all beautiful!

Phillip and Charity's Story

When Charity and I began dating, we weren't drifting aimlessly or inadvertently falling for each other. We were dating intentionally. We both had come to the conclusion that if marriage wasn't the final destination for a relationship, then the journey was pointless. I was 24 years old and she was two years my senior…I mean she was two years more mature than I was at the time. We were both passionate about serving God and serving in our local church and didn't want our relationship to become a distraction. We committed to serve the Lord together to the best of our ability. We are flawed people just like any other believer; but our hearts belonged to Jesus. After months of dating, I proposed to her on a cool starry night as we walked by the river. She said "Yes" and happy couldn't begin to describe the state of my existence.

As our affections for one another grew, our physical desire for each other followed suit. Of course this was the natural progression of a deep loving relationship, but there was a barrier in place. The word of God! We both shared a strong desire for each other, but stronger still was our desire to please God and to preserve the beauty of our wedding night. Even though I had been with a woman before, my wife was still a virgin and had saved herself for her husband…for me! That meant something. This wasn't some trivial countdown to lust fulfilled. This was the commitment made by a little girl and honored by the woman she had become. This was something to be treasured.

Chastity. Keep yourself. True Love Waits. All of these are phrases that fall into the huge bucket of "easier said than done." No, this wasn't an easy task. There were many evenings we reluctantly had to go our separate ways and many times when even kissing was a flickering spark to a pile of gasoline soaked straw. How could we keep ourselves? Was this even possible? Yes it was! With every hour of temptation, there is always a moment of escape that we could run through. Christ is greater! We encouraged each other with the thought of our beautiful wedding night. We strengthened each other with our commitment to honor God with our lives. We didn't want to be a bad example to others. We just wanted to do things the right way. I had a close friend in whom I could confide and who provided accountability and perspective; and she had the same in me. We had a great support system and an even Greater God!

Our honeymoon was beautifully intimate and without regret. Not only was my wife a virgin on our wedding day, but we walked away from a wedding that we watched God literally pay for from start to finish. It was beautiful. It was magical…and it was debt free. We had people give us money when we needed it most without us ever raising a hand to ask. The church where our wedding was held refused to charge us for our wedding and our reception. God showed us that by honoring Him, He would show himself to be a provider and a faithful Father. We're not superhuman or super spiritual my any means. We struggled; but we serve a God that is able to keep us from falling and present us blameless before Him!

Chapter Two Questions to Ponder and Discuss

1. During my espousal to my mate to be, what can I start doing or stop doing to better honor God in this relationship?

2. What family members, friends or coworkers should I stop listening to because of the wrong advice they are giving me? How do I tell them that I can no longer listen to them or hang out with them?

3. What activities are my fiancé and I doing together to grow us in our spiritual walk with God? What, if anything, is interrupting our spiritual growth activities? How can we stop these interruptions?

4.   What can I (we) do to line up with the warnings from the Shunammite girl?

5.   What steps am I (we) taking to maintain sexual purity?

6.   What lessons can I (we) learn from Nikki's story?

7.   How do I (we) apply the lessons in Phillip and Charity's story?

8. How can I explain to my fiancé that I want to wait for our wedding night, and that I am worth the wait?

CHAPTER 3

Implementing God's Plan for Marriage

*God intends and expects marriage to be a lifetime commitment
between a man and a woman, based on the principles of biblical
love. The relationship between Jesus Christ and His church
is the supreme example of the committed love that a husband
and wife are to follow in their relationship with each other.*

—John C. Broger

Most people, including believers, have misunderstood God's plan for marriage. In many parts of the world, and even here in America, the husband has taken an inappropriate and domineering role in marriage. I'm not referring to the husband as being the leader of his home; that's biblical. I'm referring to marriages where the husband has placed the wife in a subservient role. In those marriages, the wife is not his partner; she rather becomes his servant to wait on him hand and foot as well as to meet "his" physical needs.

So, just where do we begin with God's plan? God's plan for holy marriage...yes, I said holy marriage...begins with both the husband and wife being filled with the Holy Spirit (Spirit)! That's right—a holy marriage begins with the husband-wife partners being filled with the Spirit, which will cause the kind of behavior and relationship God designed for marriage. Thus the basis for marriage God's way is founded upon the husband-wife couple both having a right relationship with God through faith in Jesus Christ...they both must be Spirit-filled and thus guided by the Spirit.

As the primary instructor for pre-marriage classes at our church, over and over again I have seen couples who came to class, but it was evident that they were unequally yoked. I am not a judge, but I am a fruit inspector — in other words, I look for the fruit of the Spirit in those attending the class! In couples that seemed to be unequally yoked, more often than not, it seemed that the bride exhibited the fruit of the Spirit while the groom seemed to exhibit little or no fruit of the Spirit. There were a few times where it seemed that there were couples there who both showed no evidence of the fruit of the Spirit. Since completion of the pre-marriage class is a prerequisite for being married in our church, I wondered if some of these couples were just going through the motions in the class because they wanted to get married in our church. It seemed that some of them had the attitude of "just get it over" so we can get married. Sadly enough, I was right about some of the couples because within the first or second year of their marriage, their marriages fell apart!

Let's take a look at Ephesians 5:18-21 (ESV) to see just how critical it is for the husband and wife to be filled with the Spirit – *"[18] And be not drunk with wine, wherein is excess; but be filled with the Spirit;[19] Speaking to yourselves in psalms and hymns and spiritual songs, singing and making melody in your heart to the Lord;[20] Giving thanks always for all things unto God and the Father in the name of our Lord Jesus Christ;[21] Submitting yourselves one to another in the fear of God."*

When a married couple is filled with the Spirit, their behavior toward each other will be guided by the Spirit. For the Spirit-filled couple, this starts with them recognizing their bond as fellow believers in Christ, and thus they are able to submit to one another in fear or reverence of Christ as we see in verse 21 above. As Paul begins to teach on husband-wife relationships, parent-child relationships and employer-employee relationships, he begins by reminding us of our duty as believers to be humble and submissive to each other. In other words, as believers we are not to be insistent on things being done our way. We cannot have the attitude of many non-believers who say things such as "it's my way or it's the highway." Dr. Thomas Croskery provided the following homily from Ephesians 5:22 in The Pulpit Commentary on the duty of believers to be mutually submissive:

> The effect of the Spirit's full enjoyment is to produce a humble and loving spirit among Christian people. The principle of mutual submission, which is inconsistent with a perverse egotism or a self-opinionated superiority, has great and happy effects. It reduces the friction of human life, and contributes greatly to its comfort and peace. It has nothing in common with the servile and obsequious [groveling] temper which is such a dishonor to manhood. Let us mutually condescend to each other. The element or sphere in which this duty is to be maintained is "in the fear of Christ." This is not terror, but the solemn reverence with which we bow to the authority of our Divine Lord. Our submission is grounded in our reverence for Him, in our fear of offending Him by our airs of assumption or authority, in our supreme regard for his holy will. (pp 223-224)

In Philippians 2, Paul really teaches us about the attitude we must have as Spirit-filled believers. In his letter to the Philippian church, he taught about humility using Christ as the example. Consider the following passage from Philippians 2:1-8 (MSG):

> [1] If you've gotten anything at all out of following Christ, if his love has made any difference in your life, if being in a community of the Spirit means anything to you, if you have a heart, if you care— [2] then do me a favor: Agree with each other, love each other, be deep-spirited friends. [3] Don't push your way to the front; don't sweet-talk your way to the top. Put yourself aside,

and help others get ahead. ⁴ Don't be obsessed with getting your own advantage. Forget yourselves long enough to lend a helping hand. ⁵ Think of yourselves the way Christ Jesus thought of himself. ⁶ He had equal status with God but didn't think so much of himself that he had to cling to the advantages of that status no matter what. ⁷ Not at all. When the time came, he set aside the privileges of deity and took on the status of a slave, became human! ⁸ Having become human, he stayed human. It was an incredibly humbling process. He didn't claim special privileges. Instead, he lived a selfless, obedient life and then died a selfless, obedient death—and the worst kind of death at that: a crucifixion.

This is precisely the Spirit-filled attitude that both the husband and wife must demonstrate in their marriage. Pay close attention to the emphasis in the verses 2-4: "*²Agree with each other, love each other, be deep-spirited friends. ³ Don't push your way to the front; don't sweet-talk your way to the top. Put yourself aside, and help others get ahead. ⁴ Don't be obsessed with getting your own advantage. Forget yourselves long enough to lend a helping hand.*" This speaks to mutual submission…to compromise…for the sake of harmony and unity in the marriage!

So often with couples, one or the other try to get their way through manipulation, withholding sex, charismatic words and sometimes even the inappropriate use of the Word. So often we as husbands and wives seeking to get our way at any cost, neglect to keep in mind what agape love is and isn't…and what it does and does not do. Look at the following scripture from 1 Corinthians 13:4-7 (ESV):

⁴ Love is patient and kind; love does not envy or boast; it is not arrogant ⁵ or rude. It does not insist on its own way; it is not irritable or resentful; ⁶ it does not rejoice at wrongdoing, but rejoices with the truth. ⁷ Love bears all things, believes all things, hopes all things, endures all things.

I must confess that I really like Eugene Petersen's paraphrase of these same verses from 1 Corinthians 13:4-7 (MSG) because his words get right the point. Consider the following:

> [4] Love never gives up. Love cares more for others than for self. Love doesn't want what it doesn't have. Love doesn't strut, Doesn't have a swelled head, [5] Doesn't force itself on others, Isn't always "me first," Doesn't fly off the handle, Doesn't keep score of the sins of others, [6] Doesn't revel when others grovel, Takes pleasure in the flowering of truth, [7] Puts up with anything, Trusts God always, Always looks for the best, Never looks back, But keeps going to the end.

There are some very particular words in the Petersen's paraphrase of the scripture passage, which are critical to the marriage relationship: from verse four, *"Love cares more for others than for self;"* from verse five, *"Doesn't force itself on others, Isn't always "me first;"* and from verse six, *"Doesn't revel when others grovel."* Let's look at them in more detail. Love that cares more for others than for self, doesn't force itself on others, and isn't always "me first," all speak clearly to the very heart of a Spirit-filled believer—one who shows more concern for the welfare of others than for himself or herself. A great example of this from the Old Testament is found in Genesis 13:5-9 where Abram didn't insist on his right as the elder relative and choose the land where his herds would graze; but instead, he allowed Lot, his nephew, to have the first choice.

Likewise, a husband-wife couple who is Spirit-filled will constantly be trying to please each other, with neither trying to insist on his or her own way. The additional part of this humble and mutually submissive attitude is that neither the husband nor wife rejoices with an "I told you so" attitude, when the other admits they were wrong. Gloating over someone else's discomfort is not a sign of a Spirit-filled believer! Instead, in a holy marriage, a Spirit-filled husband and wife team will keep in mind the words in 1 Peter 4:8 (ESV) – *"Above all, keep loving one another earnestly, since love covers a multitude of sins.*" The MSG bible said it this way – "*Most of all, love each other as if your life depended on it. Love makes up for practically anything.*" Imagine that; love covers each other's faults...each other's mistakes...each other's offenses! The married couple who is Spirit-filled will operate in this manner. They will realize that they are truly one and because they are one, they need each other!

I'd like to close this chapter with the lyrics of a song by gospel artist Hezekiah Walker, entitled I Need You to Survive. Please pay close attention to the lyrics and let them speak to you:

I Need You To Survive

I need you, You need me
We're all a part of God's body
Stand with me, Agree with me
We're all a part of God's body
It is his will that every need be supplied
You are important to me
I need you to survive

I pray for you, You pray for me
I love you
I need you to survive
I won't harm you
With words from my mouth
I love you
I need you to survive

It is his will that every need be supplied
You are important to me
I need you to survive

Chapter Three Questions to Ponder and Discuss

1. Without reading further, please answer this question: What is God's plan for marriage?

2. If applicable, does your spouse to be have the same understanding of God's plan for marriage? In what ways do your thoughts differ?

3. If you had pre-marital counseling or classes, in what ways did you find it beneficial?

4. What are your thoughts on the importance and prevalence of the Holy Spirit operating in your marriage?

5. Would you describe yourself as prideful or as humble? Please explain your answer.

6. In what ways do you see yourself adhering to and/or violating the love descriptors in 1 Corinthians 13:4-8a?

7. How willing are you to truly allow love to cover your spouse/fiancé's faults? Please describe in details using actual or potential scenarios.

8. How do you see the lyrics from the song "I Need You to Survive" fitting into your marriage relationship?

CHAPTER 4

The Duties of the Spirit-Filled Wife

*Marriage is a total commitment and a total sharing of
the total person with another person until death"*

— WAYNE MACK

I HAVE OFTEN WONDERED WHY Paul began his specific teaching on the husband-wife relationship with instructions first to the wife and not to the husband. After all, the husband is the head of the home and God created Adam before He did Eve. After a lot of in-depth research, I finally had my "aha moment" and the answer was staring me right in my face. Here it is; it's because that's the way God wanted it to be! Were you looking for some deep revelation? So was I, but there was none to be found. Well, let's get on with our exploration of the wife's duties, seen in her commands to submit to her own husband and to reverence or respect her husband.

THE WIFE'S COMMAND TO SUBMIT TO HER OWN HUSBAND

We have already explored the groundwork of mutual submission found in Ephesians 5:21; let's continue looking at God's plan for the Spirit-filled wife in a holy marriage. We read the following in Ephesians 5:22 (KJV) – *"Wives, submit yourselves unto your own husbands, as unto the Lord."*

The wife's first specific duty and command or role is for her to submit to her own husband, as unto the Lord.

It's very interesting here that the wives are not commanded to love their husbands, but to submit to their husbands. We will get to the husbands' duties in the next chapter, but I'd like to address something right here. The husband is commanded to love his wife as Christ loves the church. I believe here the Apostle takes it for granted that the wife will love her husband because to respond in kind to love is already innately in her. I believe the wife will respond to her husband's love for her, and that her love for her husband, will be directly proportionate to her husband's love for her. 1 John 4:19 (KJV) tells us – "*We love him, because he first loved us.*" The bible teaches that holy marriage is an example of Christ's love for and His relationship with the Church (Ephesians 5:25-27, 29-30, 31-32). Therefore, we respond with love to Christ because He first showed loved to us. In fact, we read in Romans 5:8 (KJV), "*But God commended his love toward us, in that, while we were yet sinners, Christ died for us.*" So, God first loved us…His Church. Then, just as we as believers respond to God's love for us, the wife responds to her husband's love for her!

In order to understand this command to the wife, we have to examine the word "submit." In the Strong's Concordance, the Greek (G5293) meaning of submit is "*to subordinate; reflexively to obey: - be under obedience, be in subjection to or under.*" I've attended weddings where the wife's vows to her husband included a promise to obey her husband. I don't hear that now; instead, we use the words "submit to" which actually carries the same connotation.

In every pre-marriage class my wife and I have taught, the issue of the wife's submission to her husband has always been a sticking point for at least one or more of the brides-to-be. They see it as a negative issue and they usually voice their concerns. I don't take their concerns lightly at all… perhaps because throughout the ages, men have abused the biblical submission of the wife to make her his personal servant-slave, and manipulated her for his own selfish purposes. Husbands, if the previous statement describes your treatment of your wife, then I strongly implore you to stop it right now. In 1 Peter 3:7, we can see that the husband's maltreatment of his wife will result in his prayers being hindered or not answered…we will address this in more detail later in this book.

There's a very important element of submission the wife needs to understand. The wife's biblical submission to her husband is necessarily very different from the world's view of submission. The world's view of submission amounts to servitude or slavery. But the biblical meaning of the wife's submission to her husband is not like that of a slave. Instead, the wife's submission to the husband is where she willingly places herself under her husband's authority and protection, without losing equality with him. Her submission to her husband does not make her inferior to him; instead, a wife's submission to her own husband is her love response to him! With her submission to her husband, the wife is literally saying, "I love you so much that I am willing to submit to your authority and leadership!"

For the wives or wives to be, you have a great example of biblical submission in the person of Jesus Christ. Jesus submitted Himself to the will of the Father when He came to live as a godly example for us and ultimately in His sacrificial death. The point I want to make is this; Jesus never lost equality with the Father. In John 10:30 (KJV), Jesus said *"I and my Father are one."* In John 14:9 (ESV), Jesus said *"Whoever has seen me has seen the Father."* Now, let me take a moment for a little side note for the husbands. Our wife's submission to us is nothing to be grasped, exploited or taken lightly! Instead, we should lovingly appreciate her submission and treat her with the utmost tenderness! In fact, if our wives exemplify the characteristics of a "good wife" as found in Proverbs 31:10-31, then verses 28, 30, and 31 tells us that she deserves our genuine appreciation and praise!

Now, I believe that the most important element of the wife's command to submit to her husband is found in the last part of verse 22…*"as unto the Lord."* Therefore, the wife's submission to her husband is a part of her service or worship she is to render to the Lord. This is a very important note, especially in light of what we read in 1 Peter 3:1-2 (KJV) – *"¹ Likewise, ye wives, be in subjection to your own husbands; that, if any obey not the word, they also may without the word be won by the conversation of the wives; ² While they*

a part of your worship

behold your chaste conversation coupled with fear." In this passage, Peter was teaching the wives who had become believers after they had married their ungodly husbands...those who "did not obey the word." Peter told these wives who were now believers that they are still to be in subjection or submission to their husbands, even though their husbands were not believers. By doing so, those unbelieving husbands could be won by the behavior of their believing wives. In other words, if these believing wives demonstrated the character of Christ and the love of Christ to their unsaved husbands, then there was a good chance their husbands would be won to Christ...not so much by what they said, but by their chaste or Christian behavior.

There is another aspect of the command for the wife to submit to or be in subjection to her own husband. This command is without a prerequisite. Neither the Apostle Peter nor the Apostle Paul writes those words preceded or followed by an "if." The command for the wife to submit to her husband is not predicated on an action by the husband—it is simply her command from God and it stands on its own!

In our pre-marriage classes, I am often asked this same question; "What if my husband stops coming to church or backslides; do I still have to submit to him?" My answer is always the same...I answer their question with my own question: "Who are you really submitting to and who are you really obeying?" From a husband's perspective, we ought to be glad our wife's command to submit to us, as unto the Lord, is not dependent on our actions. If that were the case, more often than not we would probably fail in earning our wife's submission to us.

As I was completing this section on the wife's submission to her husband, I came across something that really blessed me. In an online article by US Magazine, dated Tuesday, January 7, 2014, Candace Cameron Bure, a former star from the sitcom Full House, defended her decision to submit to her own husband in their marriage. The article stated:

In her new book, "Balancing It All: My Story of Juggling Priorities and Purpose," the "Full House" alum says she has a "submissive role" to her husband, Valeri Bure. During a recent appearance on HuffPost Live, Bure defended her views on marriage. "The definition I'm using with the word 'submissive' is the biblical definition of that," Bure explained. "So, it is meekness, it is not weakness. It is strength under control, it is bridled strength. And that's what I choose to have in my marriage. I am not a passive person, but I chose to fall into a more submissive role in our relationship because I wanted to do everything in my power to make my marriage and family work. I love that my man is a leader. I want him to lead and be the head of our family. It is very difficult to have two heads of authority," Bure explained. "It doesn't work in military, it doesn't work -- I mean, you have one president, you know what I'm saying?" She further explained: "We are equal in our ... importance, but we are just different in our performances within our marriage.

http://wonderwall.msn.com/tv/candace-cameron-bure-defends-submissive-role-with-husband-i-want-him-to-lead-1790537. story?ocid=answw11

As I figured it would, Mrs. Bure's interview and article sparked numerous debates. I read many of them and although there were varying degrees of agreement and disagreement with Mrs. Bure's decision to be submissive to her husband in their marriage, I was pleasantly surprised to see that there were several women who supported Mrs. Bure's decision. As just an example of some of the posted comments, here's a couple of opposing views I found online at NY Daily News:

FROM: KIA2002

It's very difficult to have two heads of authority. Gee, I dunno. My husband and I respect each other as equals and share decision-making in our house. Neither one of us is "head" of the household, and no one is "submissive" in the relationship. We both compromise when needed. It is not "difficult" and we are pretty happy.

FROM: QNZI1781

I am a divorcee, and I do agree with her. I had this issue in my marriage, where we were both competing to be the head of household when it came to decision making and we constantly argued. I think she makes a valid point and she sees the big picture that a lot of us refuse to see when we are married. I like the comparison she makes to the military and our President...but I also feel that for this to work one of the two has to have this mentality, because if both want to be decision maker, there will be conflicts.

http://www.nydailynews.com/entertainment/gossip/candace-cameron-bure-explains-submissive-role-marriage-article-1.1569914#ixzz2pwl9sgl2

As I thought of both of these comments, and some of the others, I realized what the problem was with the women who disagreed with Mrs. Bure's decision to submit to her own husband. First and foremost, their disagreement is irrefutable evidence of their decision to disobey God's command. In our pre-marriage class, the first session deals with the Effective Elements of Communication. The last of the five elements is "Obey God's Commands." It really comes down to this: when conflict arises in a marriage, the couple must individually and collectively determine if their conflict arises from one or both of them being disobedient to God's Word. It's as simple as that.

Since we're speaking of the wife's duty and command from God to submit to her own husband as unto the Lord, her resistance to this command is not so much an affront to her husband; rather, it is an affront to God! But, there is no reason for me to belabor this point because I'm sure that the women and wives who are reading this book have a personal relationship with God through Jesus Christ...and therefore, they understand and relish the importance of the believer being obedient to the One who is their Lord and their Savior.

The Reason the Wife is to Submit to Her Own Husband

Now that we understand the wife's command to submit to her own husband as unto the Lord, let's look at the "why" behind the command. We read the following in Ephesians 5:23-24 – *"23 For the husband is the head of the wife, even as Christ is the head of the church: and he is the saviour of the body. 24 Therefore as the church is subject unto Christ, so let the wives be to their own husbands in everything."* This is perhaps one of the most neglected areas regarding the teaching of the wife's biblical submission to her husband. In our pre-marriage classes, we take great care to teach the reasons the wife is commanded to submit to her own husband. This is especially important since we live in a time where couples, especially those who are young or getting married for the first time, have a need to understand the "whys" of God's commands. God doesn't always tell us the "why" behind a command, but when He does, we can be sure He did it intentionally for our information.

The first answer to the "why" of the wife's command to submit to her own husband is because God intended for the husband to be the head or leader of the wife, just as Christ is the head of the Church as we can see from Ephesians 5:23 -- *"For the husband is the head of the wife..."* God set up the order of marriage just as He set up the order in which man and woman were created. Paul rightly taught this order of creation in 1Timothy 2:13 (KJV) - *"For Adam was first formed, then Eve."* This very definite event is first recorded in Genesis 2:20b-22 (KJV) – *"20...but for Adam there was not found an help meet for him. 21And the LORD God caused a deep sleep to fall upon Adam, and he slept: and he took one of his ribs, and closed up the flesh instead thereof; 22And the rib, which the LORD God had taken from man, made he a woman, and brought her unto the man."*

In 1 Corinthians 11:3, 8-9 (KJV), Paul also hammered home the order in marriage – "*³ But I would have you know, that the head of every man is Christ; and the head of the woman is the man; and the head of Christ is God. ⁸ For the man is not of the woman; but the woman of the man. ⁹ Neither was the man created for the woman; but the woman for the man.*" Even when God created woman, He created her as a "helper" for Adam as we can see from Genesis 2:18 (KJV) – "*And the LORD God said, It is not good that the man should be alone; I will make him an help meet for him.*"

One of the absolute worst things a wife can do is to usurp or takeover her husband's leadership role; if she does, then she is out of order! And if her husband willingly allows her to do this, then he too is out of order! When this happens, disaster for the couple is right around the corner! We can see this in the story of Adam and Eve's fall in the Garden of Eden as recorded in Genesis 3:1-7. Adam was the head of his wife and in Genesis 2:16-17 (KJV), God had given him the command regarding the Tree of the Knowledge of Good and Evil – "*¹⁶And the LORD God commanded the man, saying, Of every tree of the garden thou mayest freely eat: ¹⁷But of the tree of the knowledge of good and evil, thou shalt not eat of it: for in the day that thou eatest thereof thou shalt surely die.*"

God did not give this command to Adam's wife; He only gave it to Adam. And we know from Genesis 3:2-3 (KJV), that Adam must have told his wife because of her response to the serpent's question in Genesis 3:1 – "*...hath God said, Ye shall not eat of every tree of the garden?*" In Genesis 3:2-3, she responded with, "*²And the woman said unto the serpent, We may eat of the fruit of the trees of the garden: ³But of the fruit of the tree which is in the midst of the garden, God hath said, Ye shall not eat of it, neither shall ye touch it, lest ye die.*"

Let's dissect what happened in the Garden of Eden:

* Adam had been around longer than his wife and he had more knowledge of the animals since he had named them...
* But it was his wife who had the conversation with the serpent and she didn't have God's command to Adam correct when she told it to the serpent

- There were two trees in the midst of the Garden, the Tree of Life and the Tree of the Knowledge of Good and Evil – not the one tree the woman mentioned
- God's command was to not eat of the Tree of the Knowledge of Good and Evil – it did not include the "neither touch it" as the woman told the serpent
- Satan, through the serpent appealed to the woman's desire for knowledge to "be as gods, knowing good and evil"
- From what we know from this story, Adam was there during this conversation, but he didn't put a stop to it…did it seem strange to Adam that a serpent was talking?
- The woman ate of the fruit of Tree of the Knowledge of Good and Evil, and she gave it to Adam and he also ate of the fruit

Now if we take a close look at what occurred, we can easily see that Adam and his wife were out of order in their marriage. Adam was not the leader in what occurred; he was the follower! God had given him, not his wife, the command regarding the trees in the Garden and yet, Adam stood by while she conversed with the serpent and ate of the forbidden fruit. It's incumbent for the husband to be the physical head of his home as well as the spiritual leader and pastor of his home. God never intended for it to be the other way around.

Let's look a little further in Genesis 3:16 (ESV) where we see that when God pronounced His punishment upon the woman. He reiterated that the husband is the head of the wife – *"To the woman he said, I will surely multiply your pain in childbearing; in pain you shall bring forth children. Your desire shall be for your husband, and he shall rule over you."* The woman had taken the leadership role from her husband, which led to their sin in the Garden. Now, God was setting things back in order. God told the woman that her husband would rule over her.

The problem that often arises, especially in today's society, is that we have men who are husbands, but not leaders in their homes. Rest assured; if a husband does not assume the leadership role in his home, his wife will!

We can easily see this in the marriage relationship between King Ahab and his wife Queen Jezebel. All one need to do is read a few chapters of scripture from 1 Kings 16-21 (NKJV), regarding King Ahab's reign over Israel, and it will quickly become evident who was the head of that marriage. Jezebel was such a bad influence on King Ahab, that the recording of his reign, within only the first three verses, includes how bad he was and that he married an ungodly woman. Consider the following verses from 1 Kings 16:29-31:

> [29] In the thirty-eighth year of Asa king of Judah, Ahab the son of Omri became king over Israel; and Ahab the son of Omri reigned over Israel in Samaria twenty-two years. [30] Now Ahab the son of Omri did evil in the sight of the LORD, more than all who were before him. [31] And it came to pass, as though it had been a trivial thing for him to walk in the sins of Jeroboam the son of Nebat, that he took as wife Jezebel the daughter of Ethbaal, king of the Sidonians; and he went and served Baal and worshiped him.

Wives and wives-to-be, being known as a "Jezebel" is not how you want history to record you. That's not the legacy you want to have and leave for your children and grandchildren. In fact, Jezebel had such a bad influence and was so evil and immoral that Jesus notes to the Church of Thyatira that they had tolerated a Jezebel spirit to hang around their church. Women, let me just say this. You do neither yourself nor anyone else any good by trying to control your husband and your home! That's not your purpose or your call, and neither is that your command from God!

Now, on the other hand, when a husband is the leader of his home, it does not mean that he makes decisions in a vacuum or unilaterally; after all, God designated the wife to be the husband's helper. Therefore, any godly husband who has a godly wife will listen to his wife's wise counsel. Conversely, a godly husband has the duty to rebuke, in genuine love, his wife's unwise counsel or behavior. Wives, did that statement bother you? I meant it in love!

To help me make this point, let's look at an example of a godly husband's rebuke of his wife's unwise counsel in the exchange between Job and his wife as found in Job 2:7-10 (ESV):

> [7]So Satan went out from the presence of the Lord and struck Job with loathsome sores from the sole of his foot to the crown of his head. [8]And he took a piece of broken pottery with which to scrape himself while he sat in the ashes. [9]Then his wife said to him, 'Do you still hold fast your integrity? Curse God and die." [10]But he said to her, "You speak as one of the foolish women would speak. Shall we receive good from God, and shall we not receive evil?' In all this Job did not sin with his lips.

Here, Job rebuked his wife because of the ungodly advice she gave him. Take note; he didn't call her a fool! He told her that she sounded like some of those foolish women they had run across. And then he lovingly explained the reason he wouldn't take her advice...*Is it right that we only receive blessings from God and not have any troubles?* The very last part of verse 10 really blessed me. Job took a stand for God and he wouldn't let anyone take his focus off of God, not even his wife.

Husbands and wives, there is a lesson here. If we are going to be godly husbands and godly wives, then we must keep our focus on God and love Him more than anyone or anything else. Yes, we will address the husband's commands to love his wife in the next chapter, but even there, the husband is never commanded to love his wife more than he loves God. The Old Testament contains examples of Israel's kings who apparently loved their wives more than they did God because they allowed their wives to cause them to serve idol gods; this was even true for King Solomon. However, for us as godly husbands, we must have the resolve of Joshua: *"but as for me and my house, we will serve the Lord."* (Joshua 24:15 [KJV])

The second answer to the "why" of the wife's submission to her own husband is that, the wife is to be subject to her husband in everything, just as the Church is subject to Christ. A parallel scripture to Ephesians 5:24

where the wife is commanded to be in subject to her husband in everything, is found in 1 Peter 3:1-2, 5 (ESV) – "*1 Likewise, wives, be subject to your own husbands, so that even if some do not obey the word, they may be won without a word by the conduct of their wives, 2 when they see your respectful and pure conduct. 5 For this is how the holy women who hoped in God used to adorn themselves, by submitting to their own husbands.*" Here "subject" is used in the present participle and implies a voluntary, habitual action. In other words, the wife's subjection to her husband is not something for her to do every now and then or when she wants something. Rather her subjection to her own husband is to be her *customary and normal* action...it is a part of her worship to God!

But let's also look at the second part of 1 Peter 3:1. Wives, even if you are married to a man who is not a believer, he can be won to Christ by your godly conduct. You must not use your salvation as a "hammer" over your unsaved husband's head. Instead let the light of Christ shine through you as you submit to your husband, as unto the Lord, and watch what God does in his life through you. Furthermore, in Colossians 3:18 (KJV), Paul commands the Christian wives in the church at Colosse to "...*submit yourselves unto your own husbands, as it is fit in the Lord.*"

The last part of Colossians 3:18 indicate that the wife's submission to her own husband is "fitting to the Lord." What this means is that the wife is to submit to her husband, in honor of the Lord, as long as her husband's desires does not conflict with God's specific scriptural commands. In those specific instances, the wife is under no biblical obligation to submit to her husband; instead, she must submit to the commands of the Lord!

With that said, wives let me say this to you, although it applies to all believers. If you're ever wrestling with your command to submit yourself to your own husband, remember your obedience to the Lord honors Him, and thus pleases Him. In 1 John 3:22 (KJV), the Apostle John said it this way: "*And whatsoever we ask, we receive of him, because we keep his commandments, and do those things that are pleasing in his sight.*" Wives, your unsaved neighbors and coworkers won't understand why you submit to your own husband; however, you will know that you do it in obedience to the Lord as you strive daily to please Him!

THE WIFE'S COMMAND TO REVERENCE HER HUSBAND "How to"

The wife's second duty and command in her marriage is found in Ephesians 5:33b (KJV); "...*and the wife see that she reverence her husband.*" This is really a summation of the wife's command to submit to her own husband as unto the Lord. Here the Apostle Paul took everything he had written about the wife's submission to her own husband, as unto the Lord, and packaged it into a short phrase. In other words, in Ephesians 5:22-24, we read the "what" and "why" of the wife's command from God to "*submit yourselves unto your own husbands, as unto the Lord.*" In Ephesians 5:33b, we read "how" the wife is to fulfill her command to submit to her own husband, as unto the Lord.

Here the wife's command is to reverence or respect her husband; the MSG bible uses the term "honor her husband" as the wife's second command. To put this in a different way; a wife can submit to her husband by respecting, revering or honoring him. A wife does this by holding her husband in high esteem, and by showing him genuine admiration and devotion.

The Apostle Peter even gave wives an example of how to be in subjection to their own husbands in 1 Peter 3:6 (ESV), "*As Sarah obeyed Abraham, calling him lord. And you are her children, if you do good and do not fear anything that is frightening.*" Now, I know that in this day and time, wives don't call their husbands "lord." Peters paraphrased this verse in the MSG bible this way – "*Sarah, for instance, taking care of Abraham, would address him as "my dear husband." You'll be true daughters of Sarah if you do the same, unanxious and unintimidated.*" Wives, can we at least get a "my dear husband?"

A LESSON FROM QUEEN ESTHER

In the Book of Esther, Chapters 5-8, we read the story of a great queen who saved her people, the Jews, by showing great respect and reverence for her husband, King Ahasuerus. In fact, she demonstrated such respect and reverence for her husband that she was able to enter into his presence uninvited. The law was that anyone who came to the king uninvited faced death unless he held out his scepter. King Ahasuerus had no problem removing his disrespectful queens. In fact, King Ahasuerus had removed Queen Esther's predecessor, Queen Vashti, from her position as queen and given all of her royal estates to others. Consider the following story from Esther 1:10-20 (ESV):

"[10] On the seventh day, when the heart of the king was merry with wine, he commanded Mehuman, Biztha, Harbona, Bigtha and Abagtha, Zethar and Carkas, the seven eunuchs who served in the presence of King Ahasuerus, [11] to bring Queen Vashti before the king with her royal crown, in order to show the peoples and the princes her beauty, for she was lovely to look at. [12] But Queen Vashti refused to come at the king's command delivered by the eunuchs. At this the king became enraged, and his anger burned within him. [13] Then the king said to the wise men who knew the times (for this was the king's procedure toward all who were versed in law and judgment, [14] the men next to him being Carshena, Shethar, Admatha, Tarshish, Meres, Marsena, and Memucan, the seven princes of Persia and Media, who saw the king's face, and sat first in the kingdom): [15] "According to the law, what is to be done to Queen Vashti, because she has not performed the command of King Ahasuerus delivered by the eunuchs?" [16] Then Memucan said in the presence of the king and the officials, "Not only against the king has Queen Vashti done wrong, but also against all the officials and all the peoples who are in all the provinces of King Ahasuerus. [17] For the queen's behavior will be made known to all women, causing them to look at their husbands with contempt, since they will say, 'King Ahasuerus commanded Queen Vashti to be brought before him, and she did not come.' [18] This very day the noble women of Persia and Media who have heard of the queen's behavior will say the same to all the king's officials, and there will be contempt and wrath in plenty. [19] If it please the king, let a royal order go out from him, and let it be written among the laws of the Persians and the Medes so that it may not be repealed, that Vashti is never again to come before King Ahasuerus. And let the king give her royal position to another who is better than she. [20] So when the decree made by the king is proclaimed throughout all his kingdom, for it is vast, all women will give honor to their husbands, high and low alike."

Queen Vashti showed contempt for her husband and her King, and dishonored him by not coming to the feast as he had commanded her. Regardless of whether she thought her husband's command was inappropriate, because he wanted to show off her beauty, Queen Vashti had a duty to obey the King's command, both as his wife and as his queen. Her refusal not only showed disrespect for her husband; her actions also injured her husband's reputation as the King whose orders were always followed. In fact, the King's counselors told him that if he did not take immediate action against Queen Vashti, then all of the women of the kingdom, when they heard of Queen Vashti's disobedience, would then act the same, contemptuous way to their own husbands.

This brings up a great point for the wives. Your biblical subjection to your husband, as unto the Lord, as well as the respect or reverence you render to your husband, serves as part of your worship to the Lord. When you do, according to Matthew 5:14-16, you will be in the spotlight because God loves to display his obedient children as lights that shine in a darkened world—and you will glorify your father in heaven.

I want to close this chapter on the duties of the wives with a few last words of exhortation. In this world in which we live today, wives are faced with constant advertisements, articles, political ploys, etc., pushing them to independence and to take the lead in their marriages. However, the wife was never meant to be independent; she was meant to be dependent on her husband, in accordance with God's plan. God made Adam from the dust of the earth; but He made Eve from one of Adam's ribs.

Wives, you are destined for greatness, as long as you walk in the role God has outlined for you. Wives please re-read the story of Queen Esther. You will see greatness in her. The wife has no power in trying to usurp her husband's authority as the head of the home; rather the wife's power lies in her submission to and respect for her godly husband. In doing so, she will absolutely have great influence on him.

We can see this evidenced in the story of Queen Esther. We can also see this in 2 Kings 4:8-10 in the story of the Shunammite woman who got her husband to build a room onto their house for the prophet Elisha. A godly, Spirit-filled wife is never to exert authority or leadership over her husband. However, make no mistake; she can and certainly will have a positive, impactful, and critical influence with him as she obeys God's commands to submit herself to her own husband as unto the Lord, and to respect him. In the next chapter, we'll learn how a godly, Spirit-filled husband will fall over himself to respond to and to please his wife who habitually submits to his leadership and respects him in biblical deference.

One last thought for the wives. I read a scripture in Proverbs 12:4, which I believe epitomizes what God is looking for the wife to be to her husband. Wives, ponder this scripture which I've listed in three parallel versions...

Proverbs 12:4 (NLT) – A worthy wife is a crown for her husband, but a disgraceful woman is like cancer in his bones.

Proverbs 12:4 (ESV) - An excellent wife is the crown of her husband, but she who brings shame is like rottenness in his bones.

Proverbs 12:4 (NKJV) – An excellent wife is the crown of her husband, But she who causes shame is like rottenness in his bones.

Wives, will you be a crown for your husband or will you be the cancer that rots his bones. I know which one God has called and purposed for you to be...but which one will you be? The choice is up to you! Those around you will be able to tell which one you chose just by observing your husband! We'll know by the bright smile and aura of joy around him...or by the sadness and pain we see in his face. So, I urge you to make your husband's crown shine bright, and you will be the one who receives praise!

Chapter Four Questions to Ponder and Discuss

1. As a wife, in what ways have you really submitted to your husband's leadership in accordance with God's Word?

2. What additional steps can you take to better show your husband your submission to his leadership?

3. Do you truly see your submission to your husband as a part of your worship to God? If so, how are you incorporating this into your worship?

4. Are there ways in which you don't feel equal to you husband? If so, how can you lovingly communicate this to him?

5. If your husband is struggling in his walk with God, what specific steps are you taking to continue to submit to his leadership in your marriage?

6. How well are you succeeding at respecting your husband? How would he answer this question?

7. What is your mental or emotional reaction to hearing other wives disrespect their husbands?

8. How would you describe your husband's worthiness of your respect, i.e., in what ways does he deserve your respect?

CHAPTER 5
The Duties of the Spirit-Filled Husband

In marriage do thou be wise: prefer the person before money,
virtue before beauty, the mind before the body; then thou
hast a wife, a friend, a companion, a second self.

—WILLIAM PENN

WHEN I FIRST BEGAN STUDYING the duties of the husband and wife in a biblical marriage a few years ago, at first I thought the duties of the wife were pretty serious and I was sort of feeling sorry for the wives—until I read the duties of the Spirit-filled husband! My response then was, "God, for real... are you serious????" And in the way that only God can take our questions with humor, His answer was a resounding, "Yes!!!!" Well, that left me no choice but to seriously study God's commands to husbands in a biblical marriage. Let's begin with husband's duties listed in Ephesians 5:25-33a:

EPHESIANS 5:25-33A (KJV)
25 Husbands, love your wives, even as Christ also loved the church, and gave himself for it; 26 That he might sanctify and cleanse it with the washing of water by the word, 27 That he might present it to himself a glorious church, not having spot, or wrinkle, or any such thing; but that it should be holy and without blemish. 28 So

ought men to love their wives as their own bodies. He that loveth his wife loveth himself. ²⁹ For no man ever yet hated his own flesh; but nourisheth and cherisheth it, even as the Lord the church: ³⁰ For we are members of his body, of his flesh, and of his bones. ³¹ For this cause shall a man leave his father and mother, and shall be joined unto his wife, and they two shall be one flesh. ³² This is a great mystery: but I speak concerning Christ and the church. ³³ Nevertheless let every one of you in particular so love his wife even as himself;

EPHESIANS 5:25-33 (MSG)

²⁵ Husbands, go all out in your love for your wives, exactly as Christ did for the church—a love marked by giving, not getting. ²⁶ Christ's love makes the church whole. His words evoke her beauty. Everything he does and says is designed to bring the best out of her, ²⁷ dressing her in dazzling white silk, radiant with holiness. ²⁸ And that is how husbands ought to love their wives. They're really doing themselves a favor—since they're already "one" in marriage. ²⁹ No one abuses his own body, does he? No, he feeds and pampers it. That's how Christ treats us, the church, ³⁰ since we are part of his body. ³¹ And this is why a man leaves father and mother and cherishes his wife. No longer two, they become "one flesh." ³² This is a huge mystery, and I don't pretend to understand it all. What is clearest to me is the way Christ treats the church. ³³ And this provides a good picture of how each husband is to treat his wife, loving himself in loving her.

I was so excited about the duties of the husband that I decided to show the parallel between the King James and MSG versions of the bible. Husbands, I did so because I wanted us to get a well-rounded view of our duties as Spirit-filled husbands who are in submission to Christ. As Bishop T.D. Jakes said, "*No woman wants to be in submission to a man who isn't in submission to God!"* (http://www.goodreads.com / quotes/105615-no-woman-wants-to-be-in-submission-to-a-man)

I'd like to piggy-back on Bishop Jakes' quote and say that a man cannot properly love his wife the way God commanded him to love her, without first, having the love of God in him! A husband's possession of this agape love is never more evident in the husband's first command on how he is to love his wife. Husbands, are you ready? You will need to buckle your seat belts as this ride will be a rough one for us!

THE HUSBAND'S FIRST COMMAND TO LOVE HIS WIFE

After finishing his commands to the wife, Paul begins his commands to the husband with one that has a critical, far-reaching meaning – *"Husbands, love your wives, even as Christ also loved the church, and gave himself for it."* Let's unpack and examine this first command to the husband. The word "husband" has a certain connotation, especially in light of Paul's explanation of the reason the wife is to submit to her own husband, as unto the Lord. So allow me to start with a paraphrase of the word husband: Husbands, yes you are the head of your wife and your home, but you are not to lord your position of authority over her or be domineering!

Next we see that the husband is commanded to love his wife, and not just in any kind of way. The husband is to love his wife as Christ loved the Church and gave himself for it. This is a very specific way the husband is to love his wife. The way the husband is commanded to love his wife acts as an equalizer to the wife's command to submit to her own husband, as unto the Lord. You may be wondering what I mean by the "equalizer" statement, so let me explain further. Imagine the chaos that would ensue in one-sided marriage where the wife has a duty to submit to her husband, but he has no duty to love her in a way that brings some type of offset to his wife's submission to him. This happens and is most evident in marriages where husbands are domineering and who can often be an emotional, verbal, psychological or even a physical brute to his wife. For some men, they say they love their wife so much and that's the reason they maintain a tight rein on her – "to keep her in line." To counteract the potential for this type of behavior by a husband, we must focus on the *"as Christ loved the church and gave himself for it"* aspect of the husband's command to love his wife.

To understand how the husband's love for his wife is to be as Christ loved the Church, we need to see just how Christ loved the Church and how He showed His love. An excellent example of Christ's love for His Church is found in Romans 5:6-10 (ESV):

> [6]For while we were still weak, at the right time Christ died for the ungodly. [7]For one will scarcely die for a righteous person—though perhaps for a good person one would dare even to die— [8]but God shows his love for us in that while we were still sinners, Christ died for us. [9]Since, therefore, we have now been justified by his blood, much more shall we be saved by him from the wrath of God. [10]For if while we were enemies we were reconciled to God by the death of his Son, much more, now that we are reconciled, shall we be saved by his life.

If we look closely at this scripture passage, it is clear that Christ didn't wait for us to get it right, before He died for us. Rather, He died for us while we were still ungodly sinners! That means He sacrificed His life for us while we were still His enemies. Therefore, Christ's love for His Church was and is both unconditional and sacrificial!

Unconditional Love - This love is what we refer to as agape love. From numerous courses in my graduate programs, I've been told that WikiPedia is not a "scholarly" source for information—well, thankfully this is not a scholarly book. Therefore, I'd like to share an excerpt from WikiPedia that defines and describes agape:

> Agape, often translated "unconditional love", is one of the Koine Greek words translated into English as love, one which became particularly appropriated in Christian theology as the love of God

or Christ for humankind. In the New Testament, it refers to the covenant love of God for humans, as well as the human reciprocal love for God; the term necessarily extends to the love of one's fellow man. Greek philosophers at the time of Plato and other ancient authors have used forms of the word to denote love of a spouse or family, or affection for a particular activity, in contrast to philia (an affection that could denote friendship, brotherhood or generally non-sexual affection) and eros, an affection of a sexual nature. Thomas Jay Oord has defined agape as 'an intentional response to promote well-being when responding to that which has generated ill-being.'

http://en.wikipedia.org/wiki/Agape

As we digest this WikiPedia excerpt, there are a couple of notable things to look at. First, agape love is what God showed toward mankind as depicted in John 3:16 (KJV), *"For God so loved the world, that he gave his only begotten Son, that whosoever believeth in him should not perish, but have everlasting life."* We can see the strength and permanence of God's love for us in Romans 8:38-39 (KJV) – *"For I am persuaded, that neither death, nor life, nor angels, nor principalities, nor powers, nor things present, nor things to come, Nor height, nor depth, nor any other creature, shall be able to separate us from the love of God, which is in Christ Jesus our Lord."* In looking at Thomas Jay Oord's definition of agape, the husband's unconditional love also means that his love for his wife is not dependent on whether her actions are positive or negative—his agape response must be unconditional…period! Husbands is this hard to swallow…sure it is; but our command to love our wife as Christ loves His Church is without prerequisite, precondition or qualification… in other words, we must just do it!

Second, unconditional love refers to a covenant love that God has for us…and that the husband must have for his wife. This covenant love that a husband must have for his wife is observed in the covenant marriage between a spirit-filled husband and wife. A great example of this unconditional covenant is seen in Genesis 15 where God made a covenant with Abraham. Abraham prepared the sacrifice as God instructed. However, God caused Abraham fall into a deep sleep and while Abraham was asleep, God completed the covenant. From this scripture, we can see that God's covenant with Abraham was not based on Abraham's actions—it was all on God!

Let me prove my point. In Genesis 16, Abraham listened to Sarah and impregnated Hagar, Sarah's maid, thus fathering Ishmael. This was an act that was not in accordance with God's plan for Abraham and His covenant with Abraham. If God's covenant with Abraham had been dependent on Abraham, the covenant would have been broken by this act. Not only did God not show anger toward Abraham, God even reminded Abraham of the covenant He had made with him. But then in Genesis 20, we can see that Abraham again showed his battle with believing God's promise and covenant that he would be the father of many nations. When Abraham and Sarah arrived in Negev, he lied and told the people there that Sarah was his sister so that King Abimelech wouldn't kill him and then take Sarah to be his wife. But because the covenant God had made with Abraham was not dependent on Abraham, God acted to prevent King Abimelech from sleeping with and potentially impregnating Sarah, thus preserving His covenant with Abraham.

Husbands, we can put no conditions whatsoever on the love we must have for our wife. Since this unconditional love is an action, we must commit to love our wife...regardless. While I'm at it, let me push the envelope a little further. The love that a godly husband has for his wife must demonstrate the love of God. It is not based on our feelings—we cannot rely on the rollercoaster of emotions as the barometer for when, or, if we will love our wife! We must simply love her...period!

Sacrificial Love - Christ's love for His Church was and is sacrificial. How can we be sure that His love was indeed sacrificial? We can see that in 1 Corinthians 5:7 (KJV), "*...For even Christ our passover is sacrificed for us:*" We also read in 1 Peter 2:21-24 (KJV), "*²¹ For even hereunto were ye called: because Christ also suffered for us, leaving us an example, that ye should follow his* *steps:* [22] *Who did no sin, neither was guile found in his mouth:* [23] *Who, when he was reviled, reviled not again; when he suffered, he threatened not; but committed himself to him that judgeth righteously:* [24] *Who his own self bare our sins in his own body on the tree, that we, being dead to sins, should live unto righteousness: by whose stripes ye were healed."*

Perhaps the writer of Hebrews summed up Jesus' sacrifice for us best in Hebrews 9:23-28 (KJV):

> [23] It was therefore necessary that the patterns of things in the heavens should be purified with these; but the heavenly things themselves with better sacrifices than these. [24] For Christ is not entered into the holy places made with hands, which are the figures of the true; but into heaven itself, now to appear in the presence of God for us: [25] Nor yet that he should offer himself often, as the high priest entereth into the holy place every year with blood of others; [26] For then must he often have suffered since the foundation of the world: but now once in the end of the world hath he appeared to put away sin by the sacrifice of himself. [27] And as it is appointed unto men once to die, but after this the judgment: [28] So Christ was once offered to bear the sins of many; and unto them that look for him shall he appear the second time without sin unto salvation.

Husbands our love for our wife is to therefore be sacrificial. Just as Christ put our needs before his own well-being, we must do the same in our relationship with our wife. Let me get practical for a moment. If you're driving a nice or new car while your wife is driving a *"hooptie,"* then you *probably don't* love your wife sacrificially. If you're dressed nice and wearing the latest styles and name brand clothes while your wife's clothes are out of fashion, faded and tattered, then you *probably don't* love your wife sacrificially. If your hair and nails are neat and trimmed and your wife's hair looks like she just stood in front of a turbo fan and her nails look like she just finished a roofing job, then you *probably don't* love your wife sacrificially. Did I touch anyone's nerves? If so, you now know what to do to make things right!

Now, if Christ's love for us put us before Himself, then husbands we must also demonstrate that our love for our wife is also sacrificial. I am reminded of a news story that aired on NBC News on September 13, 2010:

> Erin Wood recalls her husband Brian as a selfless man who was counting the days until the couple welcomed the birth of their first child. And while she was filled with grief, she was equally filled with gratitude to him for sacrificing his life to save two others — hers and that of their unborn baby. The Vancouver, B.C., couple were traveling through Washington state to visit family on Friday when an oncoming Chevy Blazer weaved wildly. As the car hurtled at them head-on, Brian braked hard and swerved to the right, ensuring he would take the brunt of the crash as the Blazer slammed into them. Brian made a decision that spared his wife and their unborn child...but it cost him his life.

> *http://www.today.com/id/39146785/ns/today-today_news/t/husband-steers-crash-save-wife-unborn-child/#.U5nZGrHb6JU*

In the story above, the late Brian Wood made the ultimate sacrifice to save his wife. I believe that for the husbands and husbands-to-be who are reading this book, we too would make the same fateful decision that Brian made in order to save our wife. But honestly, even though we would make that decision, none of us really want to have to make that decision...but we would!

However, there is more. My Pastor, Bishop Kenneth E. Moore, Sr., when teaching on this very subject, asked a question that has continued to resonate in my mind. If we as husbands would sacrifice our very life for our wife, then what wouldn't we do? His point was very clear as he went on to say that if we would die for our wife, what keeps us from washing dishes, washing clothes or vacuuming? Or would you rather die than do something that for ages has been seen as "the wife's job?" Speaking for myself, I'd rather wash dishes and clothes, and vacuum or even other household chores than to have to die for my wife. In fact, I'd rather have a long life with my wife and enjoy the love that we share...so, "Honey, where do you keep the vacuum?"

Before we move to the husband's second command, a question lingered in my mind. Just what does this unconditional and sacrificial love look like? I'm sure we can all come up with descriptors of what we think it looks like or it should look like. However, I believe we get a great picture of it from a scripture we've already seen in this book, which is worth repeating here. We read in 1 Corinthians 13:4-8a (ESV):

> [4] Love is patient and kind; love does not envy or boast; it is not arrogant [5] or rude. It does not insist on its own way; it is not irritable or resentful; [6] it does not rejoice at wrongdoing, but rejoices with the truth. [7] Love bears all things, believes all things, hopes all things, endures all things. [8] Love never ends.

THE HUSBAND'S SECOND COMMAND TO LOVE HIS WIFE

The husband's second command to love his wife takes on a personal connotation. If you are a man and you're engaged to be married or you are already married, this command will definitely be personal! Look at the following verses from Ephesians 5:28-29 (KJV):

> [28]So ought men to love their wives as their own bodies. He that loveth his wife loveth himself. [29]For no man ever yet hated his own flesh; but nourisheth and cherisheth it, even as the Lord the church:

Let's unpack these verses. The first thing we see is that the husband is to love his wife as he does his own body. When my wife and I are teaching pre-marriage classes at our church, I have an illustration I like to use for this particular command for the husband. I'll ask one of the husbands-to-be to stand at the door. I then politely ask him to hold his hand on the doorjamb and I pretend to slam the door. It's amazing how quickly the husband-to-be snatches his hand from the doorjamb. I always ask him why he removed his hand and the answer I always inevitably get is, "that will hurt!" I respond with, "Yes, for me to slam the door on your hand would cause you great pain." I then turn to the class and making sure I make eye contact with every husband-to-be, I explain that just as this husband-to-be didn't want to feel the pain of having his hand slammed in the door, a husband should love his wife the same way. In other words, a godly husband should do everything in his power to keep from causing his wife any pain. Just as he doesn't want to feel pain, he should strive for the same for his wife.

Second, a husband's love for his wife is a direct reflection of how much he loves himself. Let me take a moment for a comment here. For both the husband and the wife, but especially for the husband, you must feel good about yourself before you get married. You need to resolve self-esteem issues before you get married. In other words, husbands you must first love yourself before you can correctly love your wife…and wives you must first love yourself before you can correctly love your husband!

Husbands and husbands-to-be, let me go a little further. Some of us have grown up with emotional issues that we have never dealt with. We may have a negative view of ourselves based on not having a father figure in our lives or we may have even been abused emotional, physically or sexually. I can't overstate how important it is for us as husbands-to-be and even if you're already a husband, to get help from a good Christian therapist. Unresolved self-esteem issues will play out in your marriage and can even impact your ability to be the godly leader God wants you to be. It can manifest itself as passive-aggressive behavior where you covertly abuse your wife in a way that is surreptitious and devious. Unchecked, such behavior can create feelings of fear, insecurity and confusion in your wife.

Let me close this command to the husbands with these words. Your wife's feelings of stability, security and confidence in her relationship with you will be directly proportionate to the way you love her…and thus the way you love yourself! The following story about Jennifer (not her real name) demonstrates what can happen when a husband doesn't seriously consider the consequences of not loving his wife in a way that will keep her from experiencing pain.

JENNIFER'S STORY

Jennifer and her husband came to see me in my capacity as a pastoral counselor for marriage counseling because they were experiencing severe problems resolving conflict in their marriage. Jennifer grew up in a home with a very verbally abusive father. She received professional, therapeutic counseling to help her resolve her emotional wounds that resulted from the verbal abuse. In their second counseling session, it was evident that they had made no progress and in fact they had regressed in their relationship. I asked Jennifer what she saw as the biggest obstacle to her being able to resolve conflict with her husband. She stated that her husband consistently raised his voice when he talked to her, even though she tried to remain calm and asked him to remain calm. She stated that her husband's verbal tirades took her back to when she was living under the verbal abuse of her father. Jennifer said that her husband's verbal tirades, including the use of derogatory words about her, deeply hurt her and made her feel insecure in their marriage, and also made her fearful of continuing to be in the marriage. Her husband's response was that the way he raised his voice was the way his dad had done in their home when he was growing up. For her husband, raising his voice had become the norm. Sadly, Jennifer's husband didn't even verbalize a strong commitment to change.

THE HUSBAND'S THIRD COMMAND TO LOVE HIS WIFE

The husband's third command to love his wife is also very personal and can be seen as an exclamation mark on the husband's second command to love his wife. We read in Ephesians 5:33a, "*Nevertheless let every one of you in particular so love his wife even as himself...*" The word "particular" carries the connotation of with "intense certainty"...in other words, every godly husband must love his wife with intense certainty just as he loves himself. When we picture this descriptor for the husband's love, we must with necessity understand this speaks to a passionate and assured love. We previously read in Ephesians 5:28 that the husband who loves his wife loves himself. Think of it this way; just as you take care of yourself by eating when you are hungry, utilizing proper grooming practices, and resting when you are tired, all without someone having to tell you to do it...and all because you love yourself...you should ensure the same care and nourishment for your wife.

Okay, let me take a moment here to say something, and husbands, this is probably going to grate on a few of us. This is where our previous discussion about the husband vacuuming or doing the dishes becomes important. As husbands, we can't love our wives as we do ourselves if all we do is stretch out in our favorite Lazy Boy lounge chair while our wife prepares dinner, cleans the kitchen, wash the clothes, and cleans the bathroom. Just as we all know this would make us tired, our wives too will be tired and need to rest. We can show our love for our wives by sharing in the chores around the house. This is especially true, if you both work outside of the home. Now isn't the time to get mad at me...each of us just need to do whatever it takes to show our wife that we love them as we do ourselves!

We see a parallel command for the husband to love his wife in Colossians 3:19 (ESV) – "*Husbands, love your wives, and do not be harsh with them.*" In the KJV, the word "bitter" is used instead of "harsh." The Greek meaning of bitter carries the connotation of "to make bitter." It carries a similar meaning to the father's command not to mistreat his children thereby provoking them to wrath (Ephesians 6:4). I like how Peters paraphrased Colossians 3:19 in the MSG Bible - "*Husbands, go all out in love for your wives. Don't take advantage of them.*"

In summation, we must love our wife with intense certainty that manifests itself in a passionate and assured love for her, and avoid making her bitter or hostile by mistreating her. Since I've opened the door, I might as well just step all the way into the room. Husbands, our wives will become the wives we make them into by the way we love them. At the end of the last chapter, I told the wife that she must choose, by her action to submit to (or not) and revere (or not) her husband, whether she will be for her husband as a brightly shining crown or as cancer in his bones. Well husbands, you must choose, by your love for your wife (or not), whether you want a wife who is bitter and harsh or one who exemplifies the characteristics of the Proverbs 31 wife. Remember, our wives' love response will be directly proportionate to our love for them.

ADDITIONAL COMMANDS FOR THE HUSBAND

There are additional commands for the husband that I like to call the husband's fourth and fifth commands for his relationship with his wife. These additional commands come from 1 Peter 3:7 (KJV):

> Likewise, ye husbands, dwell with them according to knowledge, giving honour unto the wife, as unto the weaker vessel, and as being heirs together of the grace of life; that your prayers be not hindered.

The husband's fourth command is for us to dwell or live with our wife with knowledge or understanding—the ESV says to *"live with your wife in an understanding way."* Husbands, this is not a complicated command; in fact, it is a truly simple command! This command calls for the husband to live with his wife and strive to understand her. That means that you must seek intimate knowledge of your wife. I've heard men say that you can't understand a woman. For those men who feel that way, I must respectfully disagree with you.

To understand something or someone, you must study it, and study it thoroughly. We must be like research scientists studying something of great interest to us. This involves acute observation and mental note-taking. We should seek to know how our wife receives love and gives love. We ought to know if our wife loves flowers or can do without them just by her reaction the first one or two times she receives them. Women have a way of telegraphing their feelings, thoughts, needs and desires. The question is this; are we closely observing our wife and taking mental notes? Are you observant of your wife's changes in mood? If so, do you wait for her to tell you what's wrong or do you ask her what's wrong or is there something bothering her? In other words, we need to be *proactive* and *intentional* about living with our wife in an understanding way!

This is as good a place as any to tell on myself as it relates to a husband's duty to live with his wife in an understanding way.

MY BLUNDER

My wife and I had been married for over seven years and one day I made the colossal mistake of referring to her using my ex-wife's name. I quickly corrected my mistake and surged forward in the conversation. However, I quickly noted a shift in my wife's demeanor...to others, it would have been imperceptible, but it was as clear as day to me. When there was a lull in the conversation, my wife went right to the place I expected her to go. She wasn't mad... she just said, "That's the first time you have referred to me using your ex-wife's name...have you been thinking about her or have you spoken to her?" Now, having done a pretty good job of getting to know my wife, I understood she was looking for an explanation and reassurance that the answer to both of her questions was "No"... which they were. There was no fuss...no mess...crisis averted!

The *Vincent's Word Studies in the New Testament*, Volume 1, page 651, defines "according to knowledge" as *"With an intelligent recognition of the nature of marriage."* This means that as husbands, we must strive to live with our wife in a way that demonstrates our perceptive recognition [*appreciation*] for the nature [*environment*] of marriage. Marriage between a man and woman is, and will always be, unlike any other earthly relationship we can have.

With our spouse, we will have beautiful days where it seems we're dancing a "waltz" or perhaps a "tango" or even a "slow foxtrot" as we move in unison…and then…there will be days when it seems like we're doing a bad rendition of the "cha-cha" or "east or west coast swing" with legs and arms moving all over the place in a chaotic fashion. But when we truly grasp the beauty and appreciation of marriage, even on those days when we're doing a bad cha-cha or east or west coast swing, we'll remember with gratitude that we were "still dancing" with the one God blessed us to be united with in a biblical marriage! Even the best dance partners sometimes step on each other's toes!

Let's now look at the husband's fifth command. The husband's fifth command has three parts and tells us 1) what we are to do; 2) how we are to do it; and 3) why we are to do it. First, we are to <u>honor</u> our wife. The Greek meaning of *honor* in 1 Peter 3:7 means *to highly value; to esteem to the highest degree; to see as precious.* Husbands, can you now begun to understand how God's plan for marriage is a perfect plan? Whereas wives are commanded to submit to and respect their own husbands, we will make it easy for them to do this just giving them the honor they are due according to God's plan!

To help me make this point, I want to share an excerpt with you of an excellent article that I found online by Patricia McGerr, titled Johnny Lingo's Eight-cow Wife:

Johnny Lingo's Eight-cow Wife

Johnny Lingo wasn't exactly his name. But I wrote it down that way because I learned about the eight cows from Shenkin, the manager of the guest house at Kiniwata. He wasn't the only one who talked about Johnny, though. His name came up with many people in many connections. The people of Kiniwata all spoke highly of Johnny Lingo. Yet when they spoke, they smiled, and the smiles were slightly mocking.

"Everybody around here tells me to get in touch with Johnny Lingo and then breaks up. Let me in on the joke." "They like to laugh," Shenkin said. "And Johnny's the brightest, the quickest, the strongest young man in all this group of islands. So they like best to laugh at him." Five months ago, at fall festival time, Johnny came to Kiniwata and found himself a wife. He paid her father eight cows!" He spoke the last words with great solemnity. I knew enough about island customs to be thoroughly impressed. Two or three cows would buy a fair-to-middling wife; four or five a highly satisfactory one. "Eight cows!" I said. "She must be a beauty who takes your breath away." "The kindest could only call Sarita plain," was Shenkin's answer. "She was skinny. She walked with her shoulders hunched and her head ducked. She was scared of her own shadow."

"Then how do you explain the eight cows?" "We don't," he said. "And that's why the villagers grin when they talk about Johnny. They get special satisfaction from the fact that Johnny, the sharpest trader in the islands, was bested by Sarita's father, dull old Sam Karoo."

"Eight cows," I said unbelievingly. "I'd like to meet this Johnny Lingo." So the next afternoon I sailed a boat to Nurabandi and met Johnny at his home, where I asked about his eight-cow purchase of Sarita. I assumed he had done it for his own vanity and reputation—at least until Sarita walked into the room. She was the most beautiful woman I have ever seen. The lift of her shoulders, the tilt of her chin, the sparkle of her eyes all spelled a pride to which no one could deny her the right.

I turned back to Johnny Lingo after she had left. "You admire her?" he asked. "She's glorious," I said. "But she's not Sarita from Kiniwata." "There's only one Sarita" he said. Perhaps she does not look the way they say she looked in Kiniwata." "She doesn't," I said. The impact of the girl's appearance made me forget tact. "I heard she was homely. They all make fun of you because you let yourself be cheated by Sam Karoo."

"You think eight cows were too many?" A smile slid over his lips. "No. But how can she be so different?" "Do you ever think," he asked, "what it must mean to a woman to know that her husband settled on the lowest price for which she can be bought? And then later, when the women talk, they boast of what their husbands paid for them. One says four cows; another maybe six. How does she feel, the woman who was sold for one or two? This could not happen to my Sarita."

"Then you did this just to make her happy?" I asked. "I wanted Sarita to be happy, yes. But I wanted more than that. You say she is different. This is true. Many things can change a woman. Things that happen inside; things that happen outside. But the thing that matters most is what she thinks about herself. In Kiniwata, Sarita believed she was worth nothing. Now she knows she is worth more than any other woman in the islands."

"Then you wanted…" "I wanted to marry Sarita. I loved her and no other woman." "But… " "But," he finished softly, "I wanted an eight-cow wife."

Johnny Lingo was, indeed, a brilliant man. He was astute enough to know that his negotiations with Sarita's father would seal forever the self-concept of the woman he loved. That's why Sarita revealed such confidence and beauty. Let me say to the husbands and wives reading this book: You have the power to elevate or debase each other's self-esteem. Rather than tear down, don't miss a single opportunity to build up.

www.biblegateway.com/devotionals/night-light-couples/2013/04/30

Husbands, after reading the story of Johnny Lingo, what value do you place on your wife? Could those on the outside looking in think that by the way you value and thus treat your wife, you feel that your wife is lucky that you married her? In other words, would others see your wife as a one or two-cow wife...or perhaps at most as a three-cow wife? Or would others, by the way you treat your wife, see her value as priceless to you...could they see your wife in the same class with Sarita Lingo? Husbands, believe it or not, we have the ability to make or break our wife by the value we place on her! The value we place on our wives will be manifested in the way we treat her. One other thought before I move on. The true value you place on your wife will be most evident to her. She'll see it best in the way you treat her when no one else is around to see how you treat her...to hold you accountable. This is where the true test of her value to you shines brightest...or is at its dimmest...when it's just her and God who see the genuineness of your heart for her!

Second, we are to honor our wife *as the weaker vessel*! This does not speak of her being intellectually weaker or in any way inferior. Rather, it speaks to the way God made her in her delicacy or daintiness as a woman who is definitely physically weaker, and yes, to a certain extent, emotionally weaker than a man. Now, let me take a moment to explain what I mean by emotionally weaker. Our wives will be more emotionally affected about issues *because* they are emotional beings. Many things that bother women do not bother men in the same fashion.

Remember the episode where I had mistakenly referred to my wife using my ex-wife's name? Well, here's the rest of the story. In quickly resolving this matter, I softly mentioned that during the entire time we had been married, that was the first and only time I had made that mistake, whereas she had called me by her ex-husband's name numerous times and I had never let it bother me nor had I corrected her. My wife responded with "Yes, but you've never called me by her name." Husbands, this is a perfect example of what I meant when I said that women are emotional beings and are bothered by things that don't bother us as men. By the way, we got through this little matter very quickly. Instead of getting into an argument and lobbing verbal grenades at each other, I simply said to her, "Honey, this is the time for us to take captive every thought that raises itself against Christ." My wife said, "You're right!" In case you're interested, this verse from 2 Corinthians 10:5, is a blessing during times like that. I'm including it below in both the NKJV and MSG; pay special attention to the last half of the verse in the MSG Bible:

> Casting down arguments and every high thing that exalts itself against the knowledge of God, bringing every thought into captivity to the obedience of Christ. (NKJV)

> We use our powerful God-tools for smashing warped philosophies, tearing down barriers erected against the truth of God, fitting every loose thought and emotion and impulse into the structure of life shaped by Christ. (MSG)

As we continue our thoughts on the wife being the weaker vessel, let's remember that this in no way makes a wife inferior to her husband from *any* perspective. Rather, it just means that she is simply different, but yet absolutely complimentary to and necessary for her husband's well-being. In other words, our wife's emotional side can often be the balance we need to make the critical decisions we have to make as a couple. After all, the wife is the husband's helpmeet or "critical advisor."

Let me add one other thing about the wife as the weaker vessel. This is an analogy which I believe will help us as husbands to understand our wife's "weaker" status. Husbands, we are like the large vase you purchase from Wal-Mart for $7.00. The vase is made of thick, heavy glass and if we dropped it on our toe, it could even break our toe. On the other hand, our wives are like the small *vase* (pronounced "vaz") that you purchase from Swarovski or Tiffany's for $600.00. Why such a difference in costs? The answer lies in the material used to make these vases. The Wal-Mart vase is made of heavy glass, while the Swarovski or Tiffany's *vase* is made of crystal. Even though the glass vase and crystal vase have similar characteristics, the crystal is very delicate and can very easily break. Therefore, the crystal *vase* is handled much differently than the glass vase. It is protected from overuse and from being broken. In other words, husbands we must see our wife as delicate and treat her appropriately.

Online I found an article entitled "Woman, God's Masterpiece." Consider the following excerpt that I believe speaks to the importance of the husband seeing his wife through God's eyes and honoring her as she is intended to be honored:

God formed Adam's body from the ground and breathed the breath of life into him. In that instant, Adam was fully aware, fully mature and totally equipped for his destiny – with one exception. God's plan was not yet complete. For the first time in Earth's short history, the Creator said that something was not good. Until that time, God had announced that every-thing He had made and done was "good." But, "The Lord said, It is not good that the man should be alone; I will make him an help meet for him" (Genesis 2:18). God knew all along exactly what He would do, but He seemed to be making a point to Adam and to all those who would follow in the centuries to come. What was that point? Work and communion with God's creation is good and right for a man, but they will never fill the special void God placed in his heart for intimate compan-ionship and completion. God's solution to fill that void was to add a unique creation taken from the deepest core of man's being who would bear the evidence of God's most delicate and refining touch. Did you notice that God's Word says He made a woman? This is totally different from the way God formed the bodies of Adam and the animals. The Hebrew word for "made" is *banah*, which means "to build, to make, to set up." God didn't just scrape together a mound of dirt to begin His work on woman. He formed the body of man from the ground, but when it came to making the woman, He began with the best of man, and with His own hands, He handcrafted and sculpted the woman. Eve, and therefore all women, have been carefully handcrafted, specially designed and uniquely customized by God to become the most beautiful creatures on the planet. That is the woman God made. She represents the pinnacle of God's craftsmanship.

*http://www.studyjesus.com/Religion_Library/The_
Family/08_GodsMasterpiece.htm*

Husbands, after reading the above article, how can we look at our wives the same way? How can we not see her as God's masterpiece and understand how unique and individual our wives are? One of the results of my understanding of how God made my wife is that my appreciation for my wife has intensified! I am grateful to God for the special and wonderful gift that she is to me!

On his Website, "Grace to You," Dr. John McArthur, one of the most renowned theologians, Bible scholars and authors of our times, provided a great commentary on what it means for the husband to live with his wife with understanding and honor her as the weaker vessel:

In 1 Peter 3:7 Peter specifically notes consideration, chivalry, and companionship. Live with your wives in an understanding way" is another way of saying, "Be considerate." Be Considerate – "Understanding" speaks of being sensitive to your wife's deepest physical and emotional needs. In other words, be thoughtful and respectful. Remember, you are to nourish and cherish her (Eph. 5:25-28).

Many women have said to me, "My husband doesn't understand me. We never talk. He doesn't know how I feel or what I'm thinking about." Such insensitivity builds walls in marriages. Be

Chivalrous - By God's design, a wife is to be the special object of her husband's love and care. As "a weaker vessel" she is under his authority and protection. "Weaker" doesn't mean weaker spiritually or intellectually, but physically and perhaps emotionally. It's not a negative thing for a woman to be a weaker vessel. In making the man stronger, God designed a wonderful partnership. One way a husband can protect and provide for his wife is to practice chivalry. Whatever happened to the custom of opening the car door for your wife? Some husbands are fifteen feet down the driveway while the wife still has one foot out the door!

Look for ways to be courteous that you know she will appreciate. Be a Companion – "Giving honor" is another way of saying, "Treat your wife with respect" while "grace of life" is a reference to marriage. "Grace"" simply means "a gift," and one of the best gifts life has to offer is marriage. Thus when Peter says to give her respect as a "fellow heir of the grace of life," he is commanding husbands to respect their wives as equal partners in the marriage. Another way to win her to Christ is to cultivate companionship and friendship. That necessitates sharing your life with her and developing mutual interests. Think about things you can do together.

One of the secrets of a happy relationship is finding commonality. These aren't mere casual suggestions. According to Peter, your applying them has a direct bearing on how your prayers are answered. Since those prayers would include petitions for her salvation, don't neglect being considerate, chivalrous, and a companion to your unsaved wife.

http://www.gty.org/resources/questions/QA119/what-does-it-mean-to-dwell-with-your-wife-with-understanding

Third, as we recall from 1 Peter 3:7, Peter tells the husbands that the reasons we are to follow these two commands is because we (the husband and wife) are co-heirs of God's gracious gift of everlasting life, *and* so that our prayers won't be hindered. As co-heirs, both the husband and wife are equal in God's eyes. My reward won't be any greater than my wife's reward simply because I am the husband and she is the wife or because I'm the head of our marriage and home.

The final part of 1 Peter 3:7 speaks to the fact that a husband's mistreatment of his wife will result in his prayers being hindered. In the Greek, the word *hindered* means "to cut out or frustrate." When I read this, I couldn't help but picture making a call on my cell phone and while talking with the other party, the conversation is hindered or impeded because it seems the call is cutting in and out. When that happens, the other party doesn't hear everything I'm saying and neither do I hear what they are saying. So communicating with understanding is hindered or frustrated. Husbands, God will hear and answer our prayers if we live with our wife with understanding, and honor her as the weaker vessel.

It is at this point that I am compelled to include an excerpt (*with his permission*) from a conversation I had with a godly, growing Christian young man named Cleophis "Cleo" Hawes who resides in Columbus, OH. We were discussing how God is preparing him to be the husband he is supposed to be to the wife God is preparing for him. Cleo said something that resonated in my mind. He had been studying about the dowries husbands used to pay to a father for the privilege of marrying his daughter. Cleo said that in the midst of his study, the Lord impressed the following upon his heart:

> The husband's pride is the dowry required for his wife. The amount of pride the husband allows God to remove from his heart indicates, verifies, and confirms the value of his wife. The payment of the dowry is continual for the Kingdom marriage to bring maximum glory to God.

Allow me to take a moment to expand on what Cleo said above. First of all, what an amazing insight from this young man who is only 29 years old! As we will discuss later in this book, pride in a marriage acts as an inhibitor to the harmony necessary for a couple to have effective communication in their marriage. As husbands, there will be times that the harmony and welfare of our marriage requires us to remove the pride from our heart that will certainly grow exponentially based on how we see the situation we are experiencing with our wife. When I feel the pride coming up, I can either allow it to grow out of control...or I can put it in check for the health and welfare of my marriage. When I put it in check, I do so from a position of meekness and humility based on the authority of my God-given leadership in my marriage. My putting my pride in check becomes my great act of love toward my wife! Husbands, I hope you also got Cleo's message to us!

As I neared the conclusion of this chapter, the Holy Spirit brought one other thought to my heart that I need to share with us as husbands and husbands-to-be. If we are really going to be able to fulfill our duties and commands from God, we must see our wife the way God intended for us to see her. We must see our wife as a "precious" gift from God! The reason we must do this is because she is truly a gift from God! In Genesis 2:22 (ESV) we read, *"And the rib that the LORD God had taken from the man he made into a woman and brought her to the man."* God formed Adam's wife and then brought her to Adam. The MSG Bible says it this way, *"GOD then used the rib that he had taken from the Man to make Woman and presented her to the Man."* The woman was a gift to the man, from the God who created them both.

The problem for many of us as husbands is that we begin to treat this precious gift, our wife, just like we sometimes do God's most precious gift of Jesus and His sacrifice for us. I believe that our relationship with and our thankfulness to God for our wife will be directly proportionate to our relationship with God! If our spiritual relationship with God begins to suffer, then it is almost a certainty that our spiritual deficiency will show itself in our relationship with our wife.

Sometimes, we get so caught up in ourselves that we don't see the discrepancies in our walk with God...until it seems that our wife is "acting up!" Then we start looking at her like she is the one with the issues... and we fail to look at ourselves. Hey, here's a newsflash! Perhaps she's just following you in the lackluster way you're following Christ! Perhaps you need to get the "two-by-four" out of your eye before you try to get the yardstick out of your wife's eye!

However, if we as husbands always strive to grow in our relationship with God and continually be grateful to God for His *unspeakable* Gift, then this attitude of appreciativeness will also show in our relationship with our wife. After all, a wife is God's precious gift to her husband!

As I close out this chapter, I want to leave this thought with every husband reading this book. Imagine what this world would be like if we led as godly men in our marriages. Imagine the health and welfare of our marriages and families if we loved and treated our wife the way God has commanded us to do. Imagine the glory we would bring to God as our godly marriages shine brightly in a world darkened by divorce and destroyed families! Let's don't just imagine it...let's start living it!

Chapter Five Questions to Ponder and Discuss

1. In what ways do you feel that you love your wife unconditionally?

2. In what ways do you feel that your love for your wife is sacrificial?

3. In what areas do you feel you're being fair with the household chores, and in what areas you can improve?

4. What steps can you take to better love your wife as your own body?

5. In what ways, if any, could your wife honestly compare you with Jennifer's yelling husband?

6. How careful are you with your words when you are angry?

7. What actions can you take to better love your wife as yourself?

8. How often and in what ways do you affirm your wife as a woman, and in what ways do you affirm your love for her?

9. If you honestly assess your wife's love for you, how would you describe it in detail?

10. If you don't like the assessment of your wife's love for you, what steps can you take to change the way she loves you, since she responds to your love for her?

11. What are you doing to continually get to know and understand your wife?

12. In what ways are you truly honoring your wife as the "weaker" vessel?

13. If you have stopped seeing your wife as God's precious gift to you, what actions will you take to change your view and attitude toward your wife?

CHAPTER 6
The Costs of Marriage

*This is the miracle that happens every time to those who
really love: the more they give, the more they possess.*

— RAINER MARIA RILKE

As we conclude Part One of this book, I am compelled to talk about
the importance of careful prayer and contemplation before you get married. Marriage is never to be taken lightly and neither is it something to
do because your friends have done it or you feel that your biological clock
is ticking faster! As I considered this, the Holy Spirit impressed upon my
heart that as believers, we must *"count up the cost"* of uniting ourselves to
another in marriage!

Again, in no case is marriage to be taken lightly and certainly,
not without some type of relevant, appropriate and biblical/spiritual
advice or counseling. This is especially true for believers because we
fall under God's commands for the start and the end of a marriage.
Therefore, we are not to do things like get married on the spur of
the moment because we are in Las Vegas like others sometimes do...
or because we are in a romantic place...or because a pregnancy has
resulted from our sin.

In counting up the cost, it is incumbent that believers desiring to get
married really understand God's plan for marriage, and their role in a

marriage as a husband or wife as commanded by God. To do anything less is like enlisting in the Army thinking it will be like being in the Boy Scouts or Girl Scouts. We find a Biblical reference for counting up the cost in words by Jesus as recorded in Luke 14:28-33 (ESV):

> [28] For which of you, desiring to build a tower, does not first sit down and count the cost, whether he has enough to complete it? [29] Otherwise, when he has laid a foundation and is not able to finish, all who see it begin to mock him, [30] saying, 'This man began to build and was not able to finish.' [31] Or what king, going out to encounter another king in war, will not sit down first and deliberate whether he is able with ten thousand to meet him who comes against him with twenty thousand? [32] And if not, while the other is yet a great way off, he sends a delegation and asks for terms of peace. [33] So therefore, any one of you who does not renounce all that he has cannot be my disciple.

In the scripture passage above, Jesus is referring to the *cost* of following Him. He uses great analogies to help His listeners understand that before making the decision to follow Him, they must count up the cost. In other words, as followers of Christ, we must be willing to give up everything else to follow Him! Ephesians 5 clearly shows the parallel between biblical marriage and Christ's relationship with His church. Therefore, when a couple decides to enter a biblical marriage, they must first count up the cost and really consider what it takes to have a biblical, harmonious, solid, and thriving marriage!

Perhaps this is a place to include a little levity. In the pre-marriage classes that my wife and I teach at our church, I usually ask the students this question: What are the three rings of marriage? They usually get the engagement ring and the wedding ring without any trouble; however, they generally have great difficulty guessing the third ring. It's of course, the "suffer-ring." Okay, it's probably a lame joke, but unfortunately many couples end up living through the suffering because they didn't take the time to count up the cost of marriage. So just what are some of those costs of marriage?

One of the things my wife and I have noticed is that some couples become engaged and set their wedding date for a year away. However, some of them don't take a pre-marriage class or get pre-marriage counseling until right before their wedding or perhaps a couple months before… or they seem to forego any kind of marriage counseling all together! In waiting so long before getting pre-marital counseling or taking some pre-marriage classes, they miss out on the true benefits of such counseling or classes. The purpose of pre-marriage counseling or a pre-marriage class is to help the engaged couple understand the gravity of their decision, what they can and will encounter as a married couple, and what being married will cost them personally as individuals. Let's look at some of the costs of being married.

A COMMITMENT TO OBEY GOD

This is the most important and for sure, the most foundational cost of a godly marriage…and yet, it is probably the one most often neglected and ignored. In order to have a biblical marriage, that is, one that honors God, it requires us to be obedient to His commands for holy living, which includes His commands regarding a biblical marriage. Biblical marriage means that we must trust God's commands…it is His Word and His way…and His plan. When we do otherwise, we run into problems in our marriages. In fact, some of the marriages in the Bible experienced problems and in some cases dire results, because either the husband or the wife or both failed to obey God. Consider the following examples:

Adam and Eve in Genesis 3 did not obey God in that Adam failed to be the leader in his marriage and instead, followed the disobedient acts of his wife. Eve of course outright disobeyed God's command not to eat from the Tree of the Knowledge of Good and Evil, and she also usurped her husband's position as the head of the marriage when she on her own engaged the serpent (aka: Satan) in a conversation. We all know the outcome of their disobedience and its impact on mankind.

Lot and Mrs. Lot in Genesis 19 were told to escape from the cities of Sodom and Gomorrah and to not look back. The command from God's angel was simple, "Do not look back!" As they were fleeing, Lot didn't look back; however, Mrs. Lot was disobedient and looked back. Her disobedience resulted in her being turned into a pillar of salt. This is an example of the importance of the couple both being obedient to God's commands. If only one spouse is obedient while the other isn't, the marriage will still be impacted!

Abraham and Sarah in Genesis 16 show us an example of what happens when both the husband and wife disobey God's command. We know that God had promised to give Abraham a son, through his wife Sarah...and Abraham and Sarah were aware of God's promise. However, they failed to obey God's command to be patient and they decided to have a son their way, through Hagar, Sarah's maid. This resulted in Sarah becoming jealous of Hagar and taking it out on Abraham. This also resulted in the disaster of jealousy, hatred and even strife that still exists today between Isaac's descendants (the Jews) and those who claim to be Ishmael's descendants.

Ananias and Sapphira in Acts 5:1-11, is a classic example of a husband and wife who first of all conspired to be dishonest with God and therefore disobedient to God. Their conspiracy led them to lie about how much they sold a piece of land for and their contribution of funds to the early church. It cost them not only their marriage, but also both of them their lives.

For us today, there are two things I want to further point out. First, as we ponder the last example, it is absolutely important that we commit first of all to honor God with our lives...in other words, we must commit to worship Him in spirit and in truth as we present ourselves to Him as a living sacrifice that is holy and acceptable unto Him (Romans 12:1). Second, since this example involves how a couple failed to honor God with their finances, I am compelled to point out the importance of us as believing couples honoring God with our finances. Even though the Bible teaches us to tithe, some believing couples have trouble honoring God in this area. I have to believe there are believing couples where one tithes and the other doesn't. In those cases, there will be disharmony in the marriage! In the cases where neither of them tithe, then the couple runs the risk of "the devourer" having free reign in their marriage and lives, as God has no obligation to "rebuke the devourer" for their sake (Malachi 3:11).

A Willingness to be a Selfless Spouse

As believing spouses, we must be selfless and willingly give up the individual person "attitude" you used to have. I realize that even now some of you as believers are having a very, very hard time swallowing that statement. Everywhere we go, we hear people say things like "never lose yourself to anyone" or "no matter what, be you." Let me just say that for the record, I'm not advocating that you lose who you are as a person or as an individual. As believers, God didn't take the personalities away from us that we each have; that's what gives us the diversities that we need in life. Instead, God uses our personalities in a way that brings Him glory.

What I mean here is that we can no longer be our *selfish* individual selves in a biblical marriage. Selfishness seeks its own way and of course, that's not love God's way. Surely we all remember that in 1 Corinthians 13:5 the Bible tells us that love, "does not insist on its own way." I find it very interesting that we can be selfless with someone who is not our spouse, but when it comes to our spouse, we want our own way...and will sometimes use deception to get our way. For example, all of us have seen a child pout, have a hissy fit or use the silent treatment to get what they want. As adults, we can often resort to the silent treatment to try to guilt our spouse into doing what we want them to do.

One of the more prevalent methods used to achieve selfish goals is the *denial* or the *use* of sex to get what we want. If you are in anyway seeing yourself in that statement, pay close attention to what the Bible says in 1 Corinthians 7:2-5 (ESV):

² But because of the temptation to sexual immorality, each man should have his own wife and each woman her own husband. ³ The husband should give to his wife her conjugal rights, and likewise the wife to her husband. ⁴ For the wife does not have authority over her own body, but the husband does. Likewise the husband does not have authority over his own body, but the wife does. ⁵ Do not deprive one another, except perhaps by agreement for a limited time, that you may devote yourselves to prayer; but then come together again, so that Satan may not tempt you because of your lack of self-control.

Perhaps some of you reading this book have never read this passage of scripture. Here, God clearly lets husbands and wives know that when you as a believer gets married, your body is no longer your own. Your body belongs to your spouse...is that clear enough? As believers we can't use excuses in order to withhold sex from our spouse so that we can "punish" him or her because you didn't get your way. In verse 5 above, we see the phrase, "Do not deprive one another." The King James Version uses a stronger word for "deprive;" it uses the word "defraud." If you are misusing sex in marriage to get your way...to manipulate your spouse...then you are committing fraud! Before I move away from this area, take a look at 1 Corinthians 7:1-5 but from the MSG. I have *italicized* part of it for emphasis:

¹ Now, getting down to the questions you asked in your letter to me. First, Is it a good thing to have sexual relations? ² Certainly— but only within a certain context. It's good for a man to have a wife, and for a woman to have a husband. Sexual drives are strong, but marriage is strong enough to contain them and *provide for a balanced and fulfilling sexual life in a world of sexual disorder. 3 The marriage bed must be a place of mutuality—the husband seeking to satisfy his wife, the wife seeking to satisfy her husband. 4 Marriage is not a place to "stand up for your rights." Marriage is a decision to serve the*

other, whether in bed or out. [5] Abstaining from sex is permissible for a period of time if you both agree to it, and if it's for the purposes of prayer and fasting—but only for such times. Then come back together again. Satan has an ingenious way of tempting us when we least expect it.

Let me say this—a marriage, and especially a marriage between believers, is no place for sexual deprivation, fraud or exploitation to get one's way or for any other reason. I am not referring to medical related issues. Ladies and gentlemen, we live in a world where Hollywood feeds the appetites of those who take pleasure in sexual immoralities, i.e., sexual sins, sexual disorders, masochistic fantasies, etc. On the contrary, born-again, believing spouses ought to see the sexual union between a husband and wife as part of our worship to God. If we believe that God cares about every aspect of our life, and that He created sex between a husband and wife for both replenishing the human population and for the husband and wife's intimate, physical enjoyment...then we ought to understand that sex in the confines of a godly marriage should honor God and therefore be seen as an act of obedience to Him...thus, it is a part of our worship to Him!

Continuing the thought in the last paragraph, it's important to note that both the husband and wife must understand the importance of seeing to the sexual needs of their spouse. The Bible clearly states this at the end of the passage above. Other acts of worship, such as fasting and praying, must by all means be dedicated solely to God. That means that the couple understands that one or both is in a time of consecration to God during their fasting and praying and therefore, one or both are giving themselves totally and sacrificially over to God...heart, mind *and* body. However, after the fasting is over, the Bible tells the husband and wife to "come back together"...that means in the intimate sexual union that God created for the husband and wife. God says the reason for this is so that we won't fall prey to Satan's attempts to tempt us! Folks, let's be clear; we're sexual beings and God created us this way!

One last comment on this particular subject; as believing husbands and wives, we must never use a "spiritual" excuse against our spouse. What I mean is this; we cannot decide to do a 10-day fast, under the guise of spiritual growth, when we know that this will bother our spouse sexually. Consider this question; if you had a strong appetite and high metabolism, would you be okay not eating for 10-days? To do something like that is nothing more than trying to use God for our own selfish reasons, and it is disobedient to His word. Let's honor God by following His Word and remembering that as godly husbands and wives, our body belongs to our spouse.

A Commitment to Let Go Pride

I have already mentioned pride in several places in this book, but each reiteration is absolutely valid. Pride can result in both bad external and internal decisions, erode trust between the couple, erect walls in a marriage and prevent a couple from really knowing each other the way they should. Pride keeps us from being vulnerable enough to share our deepest secrets, concerns and fears with our spouse. Pride will make us think we need to protect ourselves, even from our spouse. While this is somewhat expected in other relationships, in the relationship between a husband and wife, we should have no need to protect ourselves from the one to whom we are married.

Letting go pride is truly a vital cost in a biblical marriage. Pride not only prevents harmony in the marital relationship, but it is also the prelude to the potential fall or destruction of a marriage. We read in Proverbs 16:18 (Holman Christian Standard Bible [HCSB]), *"Pride comes before destruction, and an arrogant spirit before a fall."* I know we are all intrigued by the Bible story of Queen Esther who was chosen to replace the Queen Vashti, and who ultimately saved the Jews from a conspiracy to destroy them. But I believe there is really another story involved that actually set things in motion for Esther to become Queen. The story I'm referring to is really about the pride of King Ahasuerus. Consider the following paraphrased story from Esther 1 that I believe demonstrates the toxicity of pride in a marriage:

First, we see the *external pride* of King Ahasuerus. After a week of wild drinking with his buddies, King Ahasuerus commanded his servants to bring Queen Vashti out so all of his buddies could see her stunning beauty. If we read the verses in Esther 1 that preceded this event, we will see that King Ahasuerus had already shown off everything else he had in its entire splendor. Now, he wanted to parade around the one thing that should have been precious enough to him that he wouldn't parade her around for a bunch of drunken, lecherous men to gawk at and lust after... his wife, Queen Vashti. But King Ahasuerus' external pride got the best of him and he commanded Queen Vashti to be brought to show her off. However, Queen Vashti refused. Although the reason for her refusal was not recorded, Old Testament scholars have suggested that her refusal to appear was because her appearance would have resulted in lewd behavior by the King's drunken buddies, or that she was very pregnant with the King's third son, Artaxerxes, who succeeded his father as king.

The lesson to be learned here is that *external pride* can cause a husband, who is the head of the house, to make bad decisions, such as bad financial decisions in order to keep up with "the Jones." In other words, external pride can cause us to go out and buy a Mercedes Benz car when we only have a Ford car income. Now, to be fair, the wife can also exercise external pride to keep up with "the Kardashians." In other words, she goes out and buys a Louis Vuitton purse on her Aldo purse salary.

Second, we see the internal pride of King Ahasuerus. After he was told of Queen Vashti's refusal to appear, King Ahasuerus should have excused himself to check on his wife. Okay, I know what you're thinking...he was the King, so why should he go and check on his Queen...right? Well, let's meet in the middle...at least the King should have sent his servants back to ask his wife why she wouldn't come out. Perhaps she would have told him that she didn't want drunken men leering at her or undressing her with their eyes, or perhaps if she was indeed pregnant, she didn't feel well...either way, he could have gotten more information to help him make a wise decision. But, King Ahasuerus' *internal pride* kicked in because in front of his buddies, he was told that Queen Vashti refused to come out. King Ahasuerus got an attitude and he then made an even worse decision; he solicited and got bad advice from his seven closes buddies, the princes of Persia and Medes. They told King Ahasuerus that if he lets his wife get away with "that mess," then all of the wives in the kingdom will think they can do the same thing. This of course led to King Ahasuerus dethroning Queen Vashti, the mother of his heirs...and we know the rest of the story.

The lesson to be learned here is that *internal pride* can cause a husband or a wife to not talk an issue out with their spouse and instead, to seek advice from others who are in no condition to provide them any advice. The scripture that comes to mind to support this lesson is Psalm 1:1 (ESV), *"Blessed is the man who walks not in the counsel of the wicked..."* If we need to seek advice, then we should seek out wise counsel. Proverbs 1:5 (KJV) says, *"A wise man will hear, and will increase learning; and a man of understanding shall attain unto wise counsel."*

A Commitment to Let Go Family and Friends

This is an area where a lot of couples experience problems. Now before you close the book thinking that I'm way off base let me explain what I mean. This particular cost of marriage means that both the husband and wife must put their familial and friend relationships secondary to their marital relationship. For some spouses, this appears hard to do...or they simply don't see the importance of doing this. We already discussed Genesis 2:24 (ESV), *"Therefore a man shall leave his father and mother and hold fast to his wife, and they shall become one flesh."* We also already mentioned that this means the wife must also leave her mother and father and become one with her husband.

So just let me take a moment to re-emphasize that the couple must leave their mother and father and the family they grew up in, and become one in their new primary marital relationship. What this really means is that short of physical abuse, a husband or wife should no longer be able to just run back to the home he or she grew up in when a problem arises in the marriage. Some parents are more involved in their children's lives than others are and this can translate into "butting-in" even without being asked for advice. As a spouse, you must be willing to tell your parents, "I love you, but please stay out of my marriage." This also goes for siblings, in-laws, ex-laws and other extended family.

In addition, the couple must also make sure the friendships that used to be primary friendships, become secondary to the relationship they have with each other. Our spouse should be our best friend! Letting go that "best friend" relationship with someone who is not one's spouse can be a difficult transition, but it is a necessary transition. Make no mistake; friends will also intrude on their friends' marriages without being asked, especially when a spouse complains to a friend about his or her spouse. As married couples, we should avoid marital discord disclosures to friends, unless absolutely necessary for personal safety. The exception is if you know that friend will hold you accountable to God's Word!

These are just some of the basic, foundational costs of marriage. There are others that you must consider. Some costs will depend on the issues that still linger from a previous marriage or relationship, such as kids from a previous relationship. Questions to be asked include: "Will there be drama from the child's other parent;" "Is there child support involved and if so, who pays it and how much;" "Are there court orders that restrict our ability to move to another state;" "Are we responsible for paying all or part of getting the children to see their non-custodial parents for court-ordered visitation?" For sure, there are other important questions to consider. One other area that should be considered is financial costs. For example, are you willing to absorb your spouse's bankruptcy, bad credit rating, and possibly bad spending and saving habits into your perhaps stellar record regarding those issues?

As you can see, the costs of marriage can add up. But I don't want to deter you or scare you from following the path you believe God has called you to in your pending marriage. I simply want to make sure you don't go into the marriage blindly. Having all of the information you need will help you to be sure of the journey upon which you are about to embark. Stay tuned for more on this in Part Two!

VIRGIL'S STORY

Virgil and Gina (not their real names) had been married for only six months when according to Virgil, things began to change in their marriage. Virgil contacted me and said that he and Gina had actually separated…he had moved out and was back at his parents' home. I asked him what had brought this on. Virgil stated it was because Gina had started back hanging out with her friends. When prompted for more details, Virgil said that Gina was going out on weekends and sometimes staying out to the early hours of the next morning or not coming home at all. Virgil said he confronted Gina about her need to go out with her friends to bars and clubs, and Gina told him that he couldn't stop her from hanging out with her friends. Virgil sadly told me that Gina's failure to let go her incessant desire to hang out with her friends led to their separation and could more than likely lead to their divorce.

I haven't heard back from Virgil and Gina, and I don't know if they were able to work out their issues. In fact, their problem was not just an issue of not letting go friends, but they were also victims of their failure to obey God, to be a selfless spouse, and to let go their pride. These failures on their part collectively resulted in their separation and perhaps even their divorce. Not counting up the costs before getting married can be costly and result in the death of a marriage!!!

Chapter Six Questions to Ponder and Discuss

1. How adequate was your pre-marriage counseling? What benefit, if any, could you get from some proactive marriage counseling?

2. In what ways did you and your spouse count up the costs of marriage?

3. In what ways would you benefit from a written plan/agreement to address the costs of marriage applicable to your marriage?

4. What is your assessment of your obedience to God's commands for marriage?

5. What is your assessment of your spouse's obedience to God's commands for marriage?

6. In what ways have you tried to lovingly discuss your perceptions of your spouse's shortcomings with him or her, and also your own shortcomings?

7. In what ways do you see yourself as selfish in your marriage?

8. What steps, if any, can you take to be less selfish as you work toward total selflessness?

9. From the story of Ananias and Sapphira (Acts 5:1-11), what spiritual issues do you see in Ananias as a husband, in Sapphira as a wife, and as a couple?

10. From Ananias and Sapphira's story, what things, if any, do you want to start doing or stop doing in your marriage?

11. After reviewing 1 Corinthians 7:2-5 (ESV), what things do you think you should discuss with or confess to your spouse?

12. What are your thoughts on marital sex between a husband and wife as being a part of your worship?

13. In what ways have pride, yours and/or your spouse's, impacted your marriage?

14. What steps, if any, must you take to keep pride from negatively impacting your marriage?

15. What can you as a couple or individual learn from the actions of King Ahasuerus and Queen Vashti?

16. Looking at your answers to question 15, how do your answers compare to God's commands to the husband and wife?

17. Discussing these as a couple, how would your spouse honestly complete the following sentences?
    a. When my spouse and I have a big argument, he/she will call...
    b. My spouse often discusses our marriage issues with....
    c. My spouse's best friend is...
    d. When it comes to problems in our marriage, my spouse's family...

18. Think back to Virgil and Gina's story:
    a. How do you think Virgil should have handled Gina's going out to party with her friends?
    b. If you think Gina sacrificed her husband and marriage to be with her friends, what biblical advice would you have given her?

Part Two
Living Out God's Plan for Marriage

In marriage, we tend to judge ourselves by our intentions and our spouses by their actions. We give ourselves credit for thinking good thoughts, even if we don't act on them. What would happen if we started giving our spouses the benefit of the doubt, too?

— SHEILA WRAY GREGOIRE

WE HAVE ALREADY COMPLETED AN in-depth exploration of God's plan for marriage. In this second half of the book, we will look at real life examples of marriages that followed God's plan. In addition, I believe it is important to provide some practical teaching on the things we can do to have a loving, harmonious, and biblical marriage that honors God and His plan for marriage.

The illustration on the previous page gives the outline of what we will cover in Part Two of this book. As you have probably already figured out, we will start from the bottom of this illustration with the crucial foundation needed to have a marriage that honors God. We began our study with, "A Commitment to Obey God's Word" and work our way up the stairs to "Never Let Go That Hand." Again, our ultimate goal as believers is to have a marriage that truly honors God, and the plan for marriage that He put into place.

As we work our way up the stairs in our efforts to reach that marriage that honors God, I hope that you will take time to ponder what you read. The easiest thing to do will be to scan this book...perhaps to placate or satisfy your spouse...in other words, you make it seem like you're interested. Please excuse the audacity of my next statement, but if you only scan it to placate your spouse, then you will do both you and your spouse a great dishonor. If your spouse asked you to read this book with him or her, then perhaps he or she has a definite reason for doing so.

So, I hope you are anticipating the last part of this journey in which we are about to embark. I believe there are great blessings in store for all of us...and I include my spouse and myself in the "us" because writing this book has challenged and blessed us to recommit ourselves to following God's plan for marriage.

As we navigate our way through the coming words, paragraphs, pages and chapters, I hope you will have the heart and attitude that I adopted as I wrote this book. My prayer to God was and still remains that I will be the husband He has called me to be; that I will follow His command for marriage without fail; that I will honestly face my shortcomings and flaws; and that I will do whatever it takes to honor Him as the husband and the head of my wife and household!

I found out that if I lead the way as a godly husband, then my wife will do her part to "follow me as I follow Christ." Do you think these are bold words? These are the words Paul spoke to the Corinthian church in 1 Corinthians 11:1. In other words, Paul told the church to follow his example as he followed Christ. This is what I've committed to do! I will be the godly example in every aspect of my life so that my wife will see the character of Christ in me. Then it will be easy for her to submit to me as unto the Lord and to reverence me as her husband and the leader God has placed in her life.

Husbands...please join me on this journey as we commit to become the husbands that our wives will be both glad and proud to follow! Let's be the Boaz of our homes and if we do, our wives will experience the security and love that Ruth experienced! Let's strive to love our wife unconditionally, just as Hosea loved Gomer despite her character flaws.

Wives, we can't do this alone! We need your commitment to be the godly woman and wife that God has called you to be. We need you to be the highly favored wife who is pictured so radiantly beautiful in Proverbs 31. We need you to be like "Ruth" and come willingly along under the covering of your husband. And although this pains me to say, some of us husbands will need you to be like Abigail in 1 Samuel 25 and do the right thing even when we, like Abigail's husband Nabal, don't always honor God with our actions.

Let's begin our journey with prayer! Father, may our hearts remain open to you and may we strive to be the husbands and wives you have called us to be in these last days. Give us the heart and mind of Christ who came only to do those things that please you! And may we truly honor and worship you in our marriages. We ask this in Christ's name...Amen!

CHAPTER 7

A Commitment to Obey God's Word

*We destroy arguments and every lofty opinion raised against the
knowledge of God, and take every thought captive to obey Christ.*

— 2 Corinthians 10:5

We have already completed an in-depth exploration of God's plan for
marriage. However, unless we are committed to obeying God's command
for marriage, our efforts to have a successful marriage will most likely be
futile or at the least, staying together will be exceptionally toilsome. Does
this sound familiar? It should as it was the very first topic we discussed as
one of the costs of marriage. Perhaps now you will begin to understand
how absolutely important it is that married believers are committed to
obey God's Word. In this chapter, we take a deeper look into the first
building block of a biblical marriage, *a commitment to obey God's Word.*

Incidentally, as I was writing this particular chapter, I came across an
online article on MSN-Money entitled, "Why today is one of the most
popular days to file for divorce." The article went on to start with, "Happy
Divorce Day – and Divorce Month! There is a surge in divorce filings on
the first Monday of the year." According to divorce attorneys, this trend
continues for the rest of the month of January. The article contained statistics and reasons for the big divorce push. In a similar online article found
at 23-ABC, written by Lia Steinberg and dated March 4, 2015, one family

law divorce attorney was quoted as saying that the divorce frenzy activity that starts in January extends through March with the highest number of couples filing for divorce in that month. The attorney also went on to say that divorces for "the first marriage is a little over 50 percent, but second marriages are over 60 percent and third marriages is over 70 percent; so the more you get married, the more likely it is that you'll get divorced again." The article also contained a notation that the U.S. Census Bureau reported that the rate of divorce from second and third marriages are significantly higher than the first time around. I couldn't help but wonder how many of us, those in the Church, are included in those statistics.

Husbands and wives, we must understand something that is very fundamental to the success of our marriages. If we are obedient to God's command for marriage, then we have every right to expect and hold Him to His promises to bless our marriage. On the other hand, if we don't remain obedient to His word, then we have no right nor should we expect Him to bless our marriage.

I have thought about this long and hard. I have even pondered my own failures in marriage. When I brushed away all of the dust of excuses for marital separations and divorce such as irreconcilable differences, social and financial incompatibility, physical, emotional and verbal abuse, and marital infidelity, it all comes down to this: our marital failures have been and remain because of our disobedience to God's Word! I am speaking to believers! To the world, this notion of disobedience to God's Word is foreign. But to us who are called by His name, we stand convicted by the truth of God's Word.

The growing number of divorces among those who are truly in the Church is a direct result of disobedience to God's Word. I know; you're probably thinking that I just said that...and you're right. But this growing epidemic of divorce among believers needs a heavy dose of scrutiny and constant reiteration. Unfortunately, we as the body of Christ have become much more desensitized to divorce...almost as much as we have become desensitized to pre-marital sex, out-of-wedlock pregnancies, and to pre-marital cohabitation.

The matter of divorce was such an issue during the Bible days that Jesus addressed the issue of divorce in a conversation with the Pharisees as recorded in in Matthew 19:3-9(NIV):

> [3] Some Pharisees came to him to test him. They asked, "Is it lawful for a man to divorce his wife for any and every reason?"

> [4] "Haven't you read," he replied, "that at the beginning the Creator 'made them male and female,'[5] and said, 'For this reason a man will leave his father and mother and be united to his wife, and the two will become one flesh'? [6] So they are no longer two, but one flesh. Therefore, what God has joined together, let no one separate." [7] "Why then," they asked, "did Moses command that a man give his wife a certificate of divorce and send her away?" [8] Jesus replied, "Moses permitted you to divorce your wives because your hearts were hard. But it was not this way from the beginning. [9] I tell you that anyone who divorces his wife, except for sexual immorality, and marries another woman commits adultery."

So believers, has God's standards for marriage changed? Has He changed His mind? No...of course not! God said that He "hates divorce" and He has never changed His Word. In the scripture above, there is no reference to "irreconcilable differences," which is today's catch-all phrase as a reason for divorce. Here is one of the most powerful and prolific biblical texts concerning divorce from Malachi 2:13-16 (NIV):

> [13] Another thing you do: You flood the LORD's altar with tears. You weep and wail because he no longer pays attention to your offerings or accepts them with pleasure from your hands. [14] You ask, "Why?" It is because the LORD is acting as the witness between you and the wife of your youth, because you have broken faith with her, though she is your partner, the wife of your marriage covenant. [15] Has not the LORD made them one? In flesh and

spirit they are his. And why one? Because he was seeking godly offspring. So guard yourself in your spirit, and do not break faith with the wife of your youth. [16] "I hate divorce," says the LORD God of Israel, and "I hate a man's covering himself with violence as well as with his garment," says the LORD Almighty.

As believers, we do not have to guess and neither can we say that we don't know God's perspective on divorce. Let me say it again, God hates divorce... it can't get any clearer than that! By now, it should be exceptionally clear that God intended marriage to be for a lifetime between a husband (a man) and his wife (a woman). God left no room for erroneous thinking or rationalization. May I say it once more? The Lord hates divorce!

Before I move on, I must step back and say that the verses from Malachi are not meant just for the husbands because wives can also be the offending partner in a marriage and become unfaithful. Look at the following verses from Proverbs 2:16-17(ESV) which speaks of the benefits of listening to Wisdom:

[16] So you will be delivered from the forbidden woman, from the adulteress with her smooth words, [17] who forsakes the companion of her youth and forgets the covenant of her God.

Therefore, neither the believing husband nor the believing wife is exempt from Satan's attempt to make us break our marriage covenant through marital infidelity. You might be wondering why I have spent this much time on marital infidelity. It is because this is where Satan will try to tempt all of us as believers. Is this surprising? It shouldn't be to any believer because this is one of the most critical areas where Satan will focus his attacks on us.

That's why God spent so much time inspiring writers of both the Old and New Testaments to write about the importance of obeying God's Word to abstain from the lusts of the flesh...sinful passions... and sexual immorality. As I end this chapter, I'm reminded of a great example for us as believers to follow. We read of this example in Genesis 39:7-9(ESV):

> ⁷ And after a time his master's wife cast her eyes on Joseph and said, "Lie with me." ⁸ But he refused and said to his master's wife, "Behold, because of me my master has no concern about anything in the house, and he has put everything that he has in my charge. ⁹ He is not greater in this house than I am, nor has he kept back anything from me except you, because you are his wife. How then can I do this great wickedness and sin against God?

So as believing husbands and wives, we must remain committed to be obedient to God's Words. When Satan comes with his lustful thoughts and images, and he will…when he creates opportunities for us to be unfaithful to our marriage vows, and he will…we must remember what Joseph said to Potiphar's wife and that must be our cry to ourselves in order for us to maintain our integrity; "How can I do this great wickedness and sin against God?" Whether you have to say it in your own mind to yourself or verbalize it out loud to yourself and the person who cares nothing about your marital vows…we must do whatever it takes for us to honor God and remain obedient to His Word!

When we commit to obey God's Word and stick with our commitment, we can expect God's blessings in our lives. God has some promises for those who obey His Word and who keep His statutes. Consider the following passage from Deuteronomy 28:1-8, 11-14(ESV):

> ¹ And if you faithfully obey the voice of the LORD your God, being careful to do all his commandments that I command you today, the LORD your God will set you high above all the nations of the earth. ² And all these blessings shall come upon you and overtake you, if you obey the voice of the LORD your God. ³ Blessed shall you be in the city, and blessed shall you be in the field. ⁴ Blessed shall be the fruit of your womb and the fruit of your

ground and the fruit of your cattle, the increase of your herds and the young of your flock. ⁵ Blessed shall be your basket and your kneading bowl. ⁶ Blessed shall you be when you come in and when you go out. ⁷ The LORD will cause your enemies who rise against you to be defeated before you. They shall come out against you one way and flee before you seven ways. ⁸ The LORD will command the blessing on you in your barns and n all you undertake. And he will bless you in the land that the LORD your God is giving you.

¹¹ And the LORD will make you abound in prosperity, in the fruit of your womb and in the fruit of your livestock and in the fruit of your ground, within the land that the LORD swore to your fathers to give you. ¹² The LORD will open you his good treasury, the heavens to give the rain to your land in its season and to bless all the work of your hands. And you shall lend to many nations, but you shall not borrow. ¹³ And the LORD will make you the head and not the tail, and you shall go only up and not down, if you obey the commandments of the LORD your God, which I command you today, being careful to do them, ¹⁴ and if you do not turn aside from any of the words that I command you today, to the right hand or to the left, to go after other gods to serve them.

As you can see from the text above, God promises to bless those who remain obedient to Him. His promised blessing encompasses every aspect of our lives...our home, our children, our finances, and our emotional and mental health because we won't be worrying about our finances or our haters. Now, I just want to tell you that I didn't include the "rest of the story," which starts in verse 15 and ends with verse 68...these verses list the curses that results from disobedience to God's Word. Feel free to peruse them...I did...and all I could say are the words from Joshua 24:15..."*as for me and my house, we will serve the LORD.*"

So commit to obey God's Word and enjoy the fruits of His blessings in your marriage...I can tell you that if you do, you too will sing the words of the following song by Sandi Patti and Larnell Harris:

He's More Than Wonderful

He's more wonderful than my mind can conceive
He's more wonderful than my heart can believe
He goes beyond my highest hopes and fondest dreams
He's everything that my soul ever longed for
He's everything he promised and so much more
He's more than amazing, more than marvelous
He's more than miraculous could ever be
He's more than wonderful
That's what Jesus is to me!

Chapter Seven Questions to Ponder and Discuss

1. In what areas of your marriage do you fall short in obedience to God's command for marriage?

2. In what ways have your marriage become toilsome?

3. In what ways or areas are you experiencing God's blessings in your marriage?

4. If you and your spouse have contemplated divorce, what was the reason you even considered it? When you think about it now, do you think your reason(s) would still be valid?

5. What are you doing to protect your marriage from divorce, and what is your most important reason for keeping divorce out of your marriage?

6. If you have faced temptations to step outside of your marriage and engage in marital infidelity, have you discussed this with your spouse? If not, why not?

7. How important do you think it is to discuss such challenges with your spouse and pray about them together? Do you think doing this will help build better accountability in your marriage; why or why not?

8. Which one compels you the most to obey God's commands for marriage, His promised blessings or His promised curses? Explain your answer.

CHAPTER 8

Understanding Biblical Marriage is a Covenant

Marriage has the power to set the course of your life as a whole.
If your marriage is strong, even if all the circumstances in your
life around you are filled with trouble and weakness, it won't
matter. You will be able to move out into the world in strength.

— Timothy Keller

Now that we have explored the first building block of a biblical marriage that honors God, which requires our commitment to obey God's Word, let's turn our attention to the second building block, *understanding biblical marriage is a covenant*. The fact that a biblical marriage is a covenant is what makes a biblical marriage distinctly different from how the world views marriage. This is the reason why a marriage between dedicated believers must have a deeper meaning than those that exist between unbelievers of the world.

On their wedding day, a couple typically exchanges their marriage vows and pledge their love to each other for as long as they live or "until death do us part." The majority of the time, especially for those weddings where I have been the officiant and solemnized the marriage, I have seen in the eyes of the couple their every intent to stick to the vows they exchanged. So then, what is the reason for all of the divorces among believers? In this chapter, we take a close look at the primary reason for divorces among those of us who call ourselves Christians.

Marital Vows

As a part of the pre-marriage class my wife and I teach at our church, the last class covers the marital vows. In this very interactive class, we ask the students what do the *marital vows* mean to them. We've gotten answers such as marital vows are a promise, a contract, a commitment, or a pledge. Let's take a moment to examine these responses.

> Promise or Pledge - We see a promise or pledge as being somewhat synonymous and have dealt with them from this perspective: promises and pledges, no matter how intently one means to keep them, can and are often, easily broken. What we have discovered is that it seems promises and pledges are emotionally based. In other words, a person will keep or break a promise depending on how they feel emotionally about the person to whom they made the promise. These *emotions* include joy, sadness, anxiety, stress and anger. These emotions are most often the reasons couples in dating relationships go through numerous break-ups...or the reason married couples seem to be happy one week and miserable the next week...we know this phenomenon best as the emotional roller-coaster in such relationships. If left unchecked, the bad side of the emotional roller-coaster ride becomes almost constant, and the emotional roller-coaster will result in the couple becoming emotionally sick...that is, sick of each other...and they will get off the roller-coaster at the next stop!

An emotion that I intentionally left out of those mentioned above, which can also result in a person breaking a promise or pledge, is fear...fear about themselves or about their spouse. A person may fear that they can't measure up to the expectations normally seen in a marriage. This is often brought on by baggage from past relationships, especially in those where the person was the victim of verbal and/or emotional abuse. A person who was in a previous relationship where they were told they were worthless, ugly, fat, stupid…or where any number of degrading descriptors were used against them, will often suffer with the emotion of fear in a new relationship. That personal fear can, and often does, work to inhibit their intention to remain true to their promise or pledge to their spouse. In extreme cases, it can cause them to "strike first" or be the one to go outside their marriage for physical or emotional affirmation!

On the other side of that fear coin, a spouse can continually live in fear that their spouse will stop loving them and leave them for someone else. Again, this is often the result of baggage from previous, unbiblical relationships where the person was indeed victimized by a cheating partner or spouse. This fear of their spouse leaving them is so real to them that this person can become paranoid and almost paralyzed by their fear of being left alone.

These are reasons why marital vows cannot simply be seen as *just* a promise or pledge. In society's conversations we often hear the old cliché; "promises are made to be broken!" I believe that some people, unfortunately, go into their marriages with that mindset! Perhaps this is why officials in Mexico City were pondering issuing a 2-year marriage license, which would expire like a driver's license. If the couple wanted to remain married, they would have to obtain another license. Someone put a lot of thought into that proposed idea…perhaps someone who had experienced a broken marital promise or pledge.

<u>Commitment or Contract</u> – Marital vows as a *commitment* does sound good. It seems to denote something stronger than a promise or pledge. We often hear people say that they are committed to a cause and it seems that they are driven or passionate about the cause to which they have committed. How then does a commitment relate to marriage? Generally, a spouse will genuinely commit to their marriage, and will remain so as long as they feel or believe their spouse is also committed to the marriage.

This is perhaps where *commitment* and *contract* becomes intertwined. As I mentioned above, a spouse will oftentimes be committed to their marriage, as long as their spouse also seems committed to the marriage. But what happens when one or the other seems to have lost their commitment...like those commitments we make at the beginning of each year to become more physically fit or to lose weight?

When this happens, the commitment has really become a contract that requires each party to perform their part of the contract in order for the contract to remain binding on each party in the marriage. In other words, the marriage relationship has now become *conditional*. Each spouse will began to say, verbally and/or with their actions, that I will do my part only *if* you do your part!

So then the problem with seeing marriage vows as *just* a commitment or especially as a contract is that the conditional aspect always leaves the spouses "a way out." In a contract, it can still be voided even if a party believes he or she is fulfilling their part of the contract, but the other party doesn't think what's being done is good enough...in other words, fulfillment of a contract can be subjective or based simply on "how I perceive you." Is this what you want for your marriage? It certainly <u>isn't</u> what God wants!

Then how are we to see and understand marriage vows? The answer is established in the fact that as believers, we must understand that our marriage is indeed a *biblical covenant*. In other words, the exchange of marital vows results in the making of a covenant. Let's take a moment here to understand the meaning of a covenant. For sure, a covenant encapsulates the terms we have already used above: *promise, pledge, commitment* and *contract* and at its most basic level, a covenant is an agreement. Let's look at a covenant from a biblical perspective in the following explanation from the Smith's Bible Dictionary:

> **Covenant** - The Hebrew [word for covenant], *berith*, means primarily "a cutting," with reference to the custom of cutting or dividing animals in two and passing between the parts in ratifying a covenant (Genesis 15; Jeremiah 34:18, 19). In the New Testament the corresponding [Greek] word is *diathécē*, which is

frequently translated *testament* in the Authorized Version. In its biblical meaning, "two parties," the word is used —

1. Of a covenant between God and man; e.g., God covenanted with Noah, after the flood, that a like judgment should not be repeated. It is not precisely like a covenant between men, but was a promise or agreement by God. The principal covenants are the *covenant of works*—God promising to save and bless men on condition of perfect obedience—and the *covenant of grace*, or God's promise to save men on condition of their believing in Christ and receiving him as their Master and Saviour. The first is called the Old Covenant, from which we name the first part of the bible the Old Testament, the Latin rendering of the word covenant. The second is called the New Covenant, or New Testament.

2. Covenant between man and man, i.e., a solemn compact or agreement, either between tribes or nations (Joshua 9:6, 15; 1 Samuel 11:1) or between individuals (Genesis 31:44) by which each party bound himself to fulfill certain conditions and was assured of receiving certain advantages. In making such a covenant, **God was solemnly invoked as witness** (Genesis 31:50) and an oath was sworn (Genesis 21:31). A sign or witness of the covenant was sometimes framed, such a gift (Genesis 21:30) or a pillar or heap of stones erected (Genesis 31:52).

> *Smith's Bible Dictionary: Comprising Antiquities, Biography, Geography, Natural History, Archaeology and Literature.*

As we ponder the explanation of a covenant from the Smith's Bible Dictionary, I would like to point out a couple of very important aspects. First, as we recall from the meaning of the Hebrew word for covenant, it is the "a cutting," with reference to the custom of cutting or dividing animals in two and passing between the parts in ratifying a covenant. From this meaning, we can attribute the meaning of a term we use today when a new bride and groom "consummate" their marriage or "make the marriage complete by having sexual intercourse."

The very physical act of this wedding night sexual intercourse is like the final step in the making of a covenant. For a bride who is a virgin on her wedding night, the sexual intercourse with her husband equates to the cutting of her *hymen*, the membrane that surrounds or partially covers her external vaginal opening...when her husband penetrates this membrane during the consummation of their marriage. This is the reference of the "cutting" in ratifying a covenant.

Second, the other part of the meaning is the "passing through." This would still be the consummation of a marriage, and the final act in completing the marriage covenant. However, this would apply to a woman who is not a physical virgin. The act of sexual intercourse includes the passing through aspect of a covenant. Regardless of whether the bride was a virgin the night of her wedding or whether she was no longer a virgin because of pre-marital sex or a previous marriage, the covenant is still completed or consummated by the physical act of sexual intercourse, which also becomes the physical joining of the couple as one flesh (Ephesians 5:31).

This physical joining also takes on a spiritual aspect for the married couple. In Ephesians 5:32 (ESV), Paul wrote – *"This mystery is profound, and I am saying that it refers to Christ and the church."* This should complete the picture I'm trying to paint that we as believers must understand (*and internalize*) that biblical marriage is a covenant. Furthermore, it is a spiritual as well as physical covenant. Paul's words that the husband and wife becoming one flesh refers to the relationship between Christ and the church, clearly indicates this. Therefore, our marriage also becomes a part of our worship to God as we obey His commands about marriage.

So just how does this covenant marriage look? If you're somewhat like me, it helps to have a visual representation of a principle. As we try to answer the previous question, I want to share with you the following illustration, which God laid on my heart, and I believe will help us begin to see marriage as a covenant.

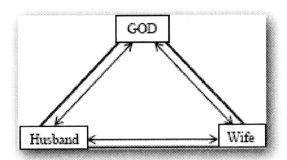

The Marriage Covenant Triangle

In the explanation of marriage from the Smith Bible Dictionary, we saw that the Greek word for covenant in the Bible means *testament*, or "two parties." The word is used in two ways. First, it is used in a covenant between God and man.

In the Marriage Covenant Triangle, we can see the arrows flowing from God to both the husband and wife; and also from them to God. These individual arrows show the covenant between God and the husband, and between God and the wife. This indicates they each individually make a covenant with God to obey His commands for marriage. That means that each of them has an obligation to God to obey His commands for marriage, which is apart from and not conditional on their spouse's obedience to God's command. Does that sound familiar? It should because it is a reminder of what we learned in Chapters Four (the wife's commands) and Five (the husband's commands), that our commands from God on what He expects from us individually in marriage does not have a prerequisite or an "if" preceding them.

In the Marriage Covenant Triangle, we can *also* see the arrow flowing from the husband to the wife and from the wife to the husband. This represents the second way covenant is used in the Bible, between man and man…or in this case, between the husband and wife in a biblical marriage. This two-headed arrow represents the *solemn contract or agreement* the husband and wife makes with each other by which they bind themselves to fulfill certain conditions (God's commands to each of them) and is assured of receiving certain advantages or benefits (the blessings of God that follow obedience to His word).

So in essence, the husband and wife make a covenant with each other, and God is the witness between them. I know; we usually have two witnesses sign on a piece of paper that they actually witnessed a couple's marriage ceremony. That's all well and good, but the only witness that truly counts is God. Why is this statement so profound? It is because if we can really begin to see that God is "the Witness" of our covenant marriage, then I believe we will start being better about obeying His commands.

Finally, as a sign of their covenant with each other, the husband and wife exchange rings. The ring is usually made of a metal that is non-perishable and is a complete circle symbolizing no end to this covenant union. For some women, and even some men, it is about the cost of the ring…the size of the diamond or other precious stone…the store where the ring was purchased…and how it looks on their finger! Now let me ask you…is your wedding ring just an accessory or piece of jewelry…does it simply say that you're married…or does it daily remind you of the covenant you made with God and with your spouse? Hopefully, it is the latter!

Previously I have mentioned how important it is for believers to remove divorce as an option for their marriage, and to not have it in their vocabulary of words spoken about their marriage. As married believers, we must truly see our marriage vows as a covenant that not only includes the agreement we made with our spouse, but more importantly, we must also see our marriage vows as an agreement we made with God.

As I move to close this chapter, let me share these words. As a married believer, you may be going through marital difficulties right now because of unspiritual decisions your spouse has made. He or she may have stopped fulfilling his or her commands from God…perhaps you have even been or you are right now the victim of marital infidelity, whether physically or perhaps emotionally due to the introduction of pornography into your marriage…perhaps your spouse has gone so far as to tell you that he or she no longer wants to be married to you or no longer loves you. If so, I know it is probably one of the most, if not the most, difficult times of your life! I want to encourage you not to give up. Even if your spouse has been unfaithful to your marital vows, you don't have to give up.

Yes, I know the Bible "<u>permits</u>" divorce in the case of adultery; however, God never commanded divorce, even in such circumstances. So again, I encourage you to continue to be obedient to God's commands to *you*! During the struggle, ask yourself if there is anything you can do or could have done better. Believe me, the easiest thing to do is to place all of the blame on the "offending" spouse. But it takes spiritual humility to look at one's self to see if you have in any way contributed to your spouse's actions, whether intentionally or unintentionally. If there is something you need to confess to your "wayward" spouse, do it and ask for his or her forgiveness. Oh, and be ready to forgive him or her!

Always remain mindful of your individual covenant with God for your marriage. When things seem most difficult and you are ready to explode, remember that God has given us His divine power for everything we need pertaining to life and Godliness (2 Peter 1:3). So above all, stick to your covenant with God and your spouse...this is how we worship God in our marriage!

Chapter Eight Questions to Ponder and Discuss

1. In what ways have you internalized your marriage to be a covenant instead of just vows promised or pledged to each other?

2. What, if any, negative emotions have you brought into your marriage that resulted from a previous relationship?

3. What fears, if any, are you wrestling with in your marriage; and to what extent have you discussed them with your spouse?

4. What issues have occurred in your marriage that have made you feel like it is a *conditional* contract instead of a covenant marriage? Have you discussed this with your spouse, if not, why not?

5. What steps do you think you and your spouse can take to enhance your marriage as a covenant with no prerequisites or "ifs?"

6. When you look at your wedding ring(s), do you see it as a wonderful reminder of your marriage, or does it have a different meaning to you? Please explain your answer to your spouse.

7. In what areas of your marriage do you find it the hardest to forgive your spouse for perceived offenses against you? Have you discussed this with your spouse?

8. In what ways have your spouse worked to resolve those issues of perceived offenses in your marriage? Have you truly forgiven him or her?

CHAPTER 9
A Commitment to Effective Communication

Love without truth is sentimentality; it supports and affirms us but keeps us in denial about our flaws. Truth without love is harshness; it gives us information but in such a way that we cannot really hear it.

— TIMOTHY KELLER

EVERY RELATIONSHIP, WHETHER IT IS a professional relationship, a friendship, a romantic relationship or a marital relationship will live or die based on the effectiveness of the communication between the parties involved. Especially in marriage, effective communication is the third building block in the foundation of a healthy and thriving marriage. Now let me quickly say this: effective communication in a marriage is not determined by the quantity of words spoken, but by the quality of the words exchanged between a husband and wife.

Perhaps one of the most interesting phenomenons in a romantic relationship is the seemingly great communication that can exist between and man and woman who are dating. Many couples experience this communication phenomenon and consider themselves to have a great relationship, especially because they experience little to no verbal sparring in their relationship. However, I believe the reason for this harmony in their relationships is because most couples when dating really don't get past the surface of honest and open communication. In most situations, couples will go above and beyond to be "nice" to each other and "bite their tongue" on issues that could later cause controversy in the harmony of their marriage relationship.

Let me even go as far as to say that some couples get married when they shouldn't have, and it's because they were not open and honest about their communication. Sometimes we want someone in our life so bad that we will ignore serious issues and bite our tongues on those issues that we need to bring out into the open. This is as good a place as any to tell my story. I'm about to be vulnerable here, so please show me some mercy!

My Story

In late 2006, I met a woman through a Christian dating website that was called Relationships; it is now ChristianMingle. We talked online and by phone for a few months before I traveled to visit her. After meeting her in person, it seemed that we would be a good fit. But then, I began to notice some things that begin to make me question the relationship. For example, it seemed that she always made an excuse when it was time to go to church. In addition, she had married friends who she spent time with who openly told her about their extra-marital affairs...however, she didn't distance herself from them. She discussed things with her single friends involving their sexual escapades, which should have made her withdraw from them.

But I digress because this is about me. I saw those things and I heard those things, but I kept my mouth shut because I wanted some-one...and I thought that someone was her. The fault is mine...not hers! I'm the one who saw the issues clearly; yet I remained silent while hoping things would change...they didn't. This is what made it worse; she brought up minor things that bothered her...yet I kept silent about major issues. The stop signs were all there, but I blew through them because I wanted someone in my life...and I thought it was her...at the time, I wanted it to be her! But then things got worse...we got engaged and each time we tried to schedule the wedding, something happened to stop us. Finally, like the prodigal son in the pig's pen, I came to myself...to my senses. God gave me the moment of clarity I needed! I told God that if she was not the one for me, then I wanted Him to put up one more stop sign and I promised Him that I wouldn't go through it. True to the God who has called and purposed the life of every believer, God put up a gigantic stop sign. I used to wonder why He put up such a large stop sign... and then I realized He did that because He knows me...and He knew that if it wasn't the size of Texas, then I would have tried to go around it...but this stop sign left me no choice...God didn't leave it up to me...and for that, I am so grateful to Him!!!

What I learned the most from that doomed relationship was that it is absolutely critical that a relationship includes open and honest communication! To do otherwise is unfair to you as well as to the other person in the relationship with you. This became even more real for me as I studied God's plan for marriage and especially my responsibility as the husband. We'll talk more about this in later in this chapter, but I learned that I must be the voice of warning in my marriage...and in my home. I cannot just sit idly by and watch my wife or our children make decisions and follow paths that are outside of God's commands...I must speak up! When I do, I truly show how much I love them...if I don't, then that pretty much means that I don't love them enough to want them to experience God's best for them...or that I don't care enough about them to keep them from experiencing God's wrath or discipline in their life. It's more important that we as husbands put aside our worrying about being in the "dog house" with our wives or not being seen as a "cool dad" to our children, and instead speak the truth to them in love. Speaking up against sin is not always popular, but as the head of our homes, husbands we are the watchmen on the gate. We must first fortify ourselves against the danger, and then guard ourselves and our families against that "roaring lion" who is on the prowl looking to destroy us.

EFFECTIVE COMMUNICATION STARTS WITH BEING EQUALLY YOKED

I had planned to start with another topic, but I became keenly aware of this pressing feeling in my heart to start with being equally yoked. First of all, if you are a believer, you should not be looking at an unbeliever as your potential spouse. Let me just say it loud and clear; if you are a believer and you are engaged to an unbeliever, you are asking for a very troubled marriage! How can you even hope to have a strong footing for your marriage? Now, if you became a believer after you were already married and your spouse has remained an unbeliever, then that's an entirely different story and the Bible addresses that situation very clearly in 1 Corinthians 7:12-16 (ESV):

> [12] To the rest I say (I, not the Lord) that if any brother has a wife who is an unbeliever, and she consents to live with him, he should not divorce her. [13] If any woman has a husband who is an unbeliever, and he consents to live with her, she should not divorce him. [14] For the unbelieving husband is made holy because of his wife, and the unbelieving wife is made holy because of her husband. Otherwise your children would be unclean, but as it is, they are holy. [15] But if the unbelieving partner separates, let it be so. In such cases the brother or sister is not enslaved. God has called you to peace. [16] For how do you know, wife, whether you will save your husband? Or how do you know, husband, whether you will save your wife?

So as a believer married to an unbeliever, it is absolutely essential that you live according to God's commands for marriage so that by your obedience to God, you can draw your unbelieving spouse into a personal relationship with Christ.

Now, let's return to the subject of being equally yoked and its importance in a married couple's effective communication. It's also important to note that effective communication builds upon the couple's commitment to obey God's Word in a biblical covenant marriage, and thus becomes the next layer upon which a strong, thriving and sizzling marriage is built. Are you asking yourself why I emphasized the importance of being equally yoked and its subsequent importance on effective communication? Let's look at a two quick reasons, which I believe will answer your question.

First, being equally yoked with another believer in marriage means that each spouse should have an expectation that the other is not only committed to being obedient to God's Word regarding marriage, but is also committed to being obedient to His Word regarding relationships between believers.

I think that spouses sometimes forget...or perhaps we simply choose to ignore what the Bible tells us how to get along with our brothers and sisters in Christ. We must never forget that our believing spouse is first and foremost a child of God, and in essence, that alone should govern how we treat them and talk to them. I know...some of you have smirks on your faces or have scrunched up your faces in your "I don't think so" disagreement with me. Well, what does the Bible say about how we treat our brothers and sisters, including how we talk to them? Take a look at the following scriptures:

Proverbs 15:1, 18 (ESV) – [1] A soft answer turns away wrath, but a harsh word stirs up anger. [18] A hot-tempered man stirs up strife, but he who is slow to anger quiets contention.

John 13:34-35 (ESV) – [34] A new commandment I give to you, that you love one another: just as I have loved you, you also are to love one another. [35] By this all people will know that you are my disciples, if you have love for one another.

Mark 12:31 (ESV) – [31] The second is this: 'You shall love your neighbor as yourself.' There is no other commandment greater than these.

Ephesians 4:29-32 (ESV) – [29] Let no corrupting talk come out of your mouths, but only such as is good for building up, as fits the occasion, that it may give grace to those who hear. [30] And do not grieve the Holy Spirit of God, by whom you were sealed for the day of redemption. [31] Let all bitterness and wrath and anger and clamor and slander be put away from you, along with all malice. [32] Be kind to one another, tenderhearted, forgiving one another, as God in Christ forgave you.

1 Peter 3:8-12 (ESV) – [8] Finally, all of you, have unity of mind, sympathy, brotherly love, a tender heart, and a humble mind. [9] Do not repay evil for evil or reviling for reviling, but on the contrary, bless, for to this you were called, that you may obtain a blessing. [10] For "Whoever desires to love life and see good days, let him keep his tongue from evil and his lips from speaking deceit; [11] let him turn away from evil and do good; let him seek peace and pursue it. [12] For the eyes of the Lord are on the righteous, and his ears are open to their prayer. But the face of the Lord is against those who do evil.

Colossians 3:12-14 (ESV) – [12] Put on then, as God's chosen ones, holy and beloved, compassionate hearts, kindness, humility, meekness, and patience, [13] bearing with one another and, if one has a complaint against another, forgiving each other; as the Lord has forgiven you, so you also must forgive. [14] And above all these put on love, which binds everything together in perfect harmony.

1 Corinthians 13:4-8a (ESV) – [4] Love is patient and kind; love does not envy or boast; it is not arrogant [5] or rude. It does not insist on its own way; it is not irritable or resentful; [6] it does not rejoice at wrongdoing, but rejoices with the truth. [7] Love bears all things, believes all things, hopes all things, endures all things. [8] Love never ends.

From the scriptures above, it is clear that as married believers, we still have a biblical responsibility to treat each other with the love of Christ. You might be thinking that you can't just do that...sometimes you get "hot" and have to tell it like it is…with harsh words and a loud volume! I beg to differ with you. In fact, in 1 Corinthians 5:14, the Apostle Paul wrote that *"the love of Christ constrained"* him, which compelled him to do with one focus what Christ wanted him to do. In other words, when we focus on being obedient to Christ, this will supersede our misplaced desire to do or say things our own way. Furthermore, being married to your brother or sister in Christ does not in the least negate our Christ-like love responsibility to each other or allow us to speak harshly to each other. Since we have established this point, let's look at the next one.

Second, being equally yoked with another believer in marriage, means that each spouse *will have* the power and will *have* (or at least *should have*) the desire to adhere to God's Word. This means that each person will understand that a marriage God's way requires adherence to His Word. The equally yoked couple can read God's Word and follow it because as Spirit-filled believers, they would have both *the desire and the power*, to obey God's Word. Allow me to prove this point from God's Word. In and of ourselves, we may have the desire to do the right thing in our marriage, but without the Spirit, we won't have the power! We need both!

How then do we reach this plateau of having both desire and power to obey God's Word for marriage? Paul tells us that we reach this plateau because of God's grace. Here it is from in 1 Corinthians 15:10 (NLT): *"But whatever I am now, it is all because God poured out his special favor on me—and not without results. For I have worked harder than any of the other apostles; yet it was not I but God who was working through me by his grace."*

There is no way that we can even remotely do this on our own…that is, have a Godly marriage…one that honors the very essence and the spirit of God's command's for marriage! Looking in 2 Corinthians 3:5 (ESV), we see that Paul said this about the successes that follow those who adhere to God's will for their lives – *"Not that we are sufficient in ourselves to claim anything as coming from us, but our sufficiency is from God…"* Hey, here's a wake-up call; you are not doing it on your own…it's all God! We read in Philippians 2:13 (NLT) – *"For God is working in you, giving you the desire to obey him and the power to do what pleases him."*

An unbeliever would certainly not have the same power to obey God, and most likely, neither would he or she have the desire to obey God's Word to its fullest extent…to fight against the flesh! Can you imagine what kind of havoc that would cause in your marriage? Even as Spirit-filled believers, we struggle with and war against the flesh…the lusts of the flesh, the lusts of the eyes and the pride of life are our constant enemies! So what power does the unbeliever have to not fall victim to this onslaught…or what desire will they have to even fight those sensual, temporary pleasures of the flesh? In fact, they have no obligation to be obedient to God's Word because they are not His children! A husband who is not a believer will not have any obligation to love his wife as Christ loves the church, as he does his own body or as he does himself! A wife who is not a believer will have no obligation to submit herself to her own husband as unto the Lord or to respect her husband!

As a believer, is this the outcome you want in your marriage, especially since you now know the content of God's plan for marriage? For the believer who intends to go ahead and marry an unbeliever, you may want to first consider having brain surgery…and without the use of any anesthetic! What I mean is this; the emotional pain you're headed for will be extremely severe and as my pastor Bishop Kenneth More, Sr. often says, "It'll make you lose your mind!" I think that every believer who is in an equally yoked marriage would agree with me on this: for a believer to enter be into an unequally yoked marriage would be a very *stupid* decision! Did I offend you by using the word stupid? If so, consider its meaning:

Stupid - foolish, unintelligent, idiotic, nonsensical, senseless, harebrained, unthinking, ill-advised, ill-considered, unwise, injudicious; absurd, ridiculous, insane, lunatic.

The preceding words used to describe stupid have a common theme. They all indicate something a person does that is unwise and without either listening to wise counsel or simply ignoring wise counsel. Believe me; as Christians in equally yoked marriages we still have our share of problems in our marriages. Speaking strictly for myself as a believer; I know for sure that if I were not already married, I would never consider marriage to an unbeliever!

Again, let me reiterate that if you became a believer after you were already married, and your spouse has not yet become a believer, you are obligated to remain married to your spouse, as long as he or she wants to remain married to you. If that's your situation, then just remember that God's grace is sufficient for you to see you through each situation that you encounter in your marriage.

EFFECTIVE COMMUNICATION REQUIRES US TO RESPECT EACH OTHER

This is not some deep, philosophical concept...it is simply treating your spouse as you want to be treated! In fact, the Bible tells us in Luke 6:31 (NLT) to "*Do to others as you would like them to do to you.*" One of the biggest inhibitors to effective communication in a marriage is the lack of mutual respect. Oftentimes, husbands will insist on his wife showing him respect in accordance with her command in Ephesians 5:33b (NLT) which states, "*and the wife must respect her husband.*" However, those same husbands seem to have forgotten or simply have neglected the command in Ephesians 5:21 (NLT) which states, "*And further, you will submit to one another out of reverence for Christ.*" In a biblical marriage, the husband and wife must respect each other!

Dr. David Hawkins of The Marriage Recovery Center, in an online article dated June 24, 2013 and titled, *The Importance of Mutual Respect,* stated that he has found that "a common thread in relationships is a desire for mutual respect." He provided the following suggestions to help couples in their relationships:

First, *mutual respect is a foundation for any relationship.* While infusing our relationships with respect may be challenging, and at times hard to define, it is critical for any healthy relationship. Generally, respect is present when we embrace the concepts of acceptance, forgiveness, allowing another to make mistakes without judging their motives, listening and appreciating their unique personality. We treat others honorably, listening to them and valuing their points of view. We are sensitive to the boundaries they have established.

Second, *mutual respect can be damaged and must be repaired.* In the natural ebb and flow of life we will, often without malicious motives, harm the respect of another. We do this by pushing our point of view onto another, by violating their boundaries, spoken and unspoken, and by not accepting their personhood.

Third, *rebuilding mutual respect will take time and effort.* Once we have violated another, we've broken their trust. It is natural to withdraw into a shell of protectiveness, often developing feelings of bitterness, and this breaks healthy connection. It is critical that we talk about what we need to feel respected, how others violate those boundaries, and how you can work together to rebuild respect.

Finally, *mutual respect must be maintained together.* Both partners must commit to infusing their relationship with mutual respect. This is done by clarifying boundaries, needs and wishes. Others cannot read our minds and often don't know they are harming us. Attend to what causes empathy and connection and work toward it. Show your mate that you care enough to attend to their concerns.

http://www.crosswalk.com/family/marriage/doctor-david/the-importance-of-mutual-respect.html

I agree with Dr. Hawkin's perspectives on mutual submission in marriage. Let me take a moment to speak directly to the husbands and the husbands-to-be. It is imperative that we model this mutual respect in our relationship with our wife or wife-to-be. Each of us can best model this in our role as a servant-leader in our relationship. Men if you're thinking it's the wife's duty to respect you and that you have no duty to respect her then I urge you to go back to God's first command to the husband. The husband is to love his wife as Christ loves the church, which is unconditionally and sacrificially. The concept of sacrificial love includes putting another before yourself, and it becomes exponentially easier to do that when you respect the person, and if you're going to do it genuinely!

As a believer, whether already married or waiting to be married, I urge you to respect your God-given mate. If you do this, you will see the harmony and communication in your relationship grow to another level.

EFFECTIVE COMMUNICATION REQUIRES US TO LET OUR PRIDE GO

One of the most devastating things in a marriage is pride! Let me be more specific; I am referring to the negative aspect of pride. The positive aspect of pride can be healthy for an individual as well as for a couple. For example, a couple can have pride in certain goals they have accomplished as they have followed God's plan for marriage, or an individual can take pride in having reached their goal of weight loss or having earned a college degree. This type of pride helps an individual or a couple's self-esteem. In other words, it provides them with an appreciative and positive, but non-arrogant view of themselves.

On the other hand, the negative aspect of pride, whether displayed by the husband or the wife, can bring your marriage to a screeching halt! This aspect of pride is absolutely debilitating to the harmony and effective communication in the marriage relationship. Let's look at a definition of this type of pride. Dictionary.com displayed the following definition of the negative aspect of *pride*:

High or inordinate opinion of one's own dignity, importance, merit, or superiority, whether as cherished in the mind or as displayed in bearing, conduct, etc.

I believe the key word in this definition is *inordinate*. If we look at this word in a thesaurus, we find other words to help us understand its meaning – *"excessive, undue, unwarranted, extravagant, unreasonable, disproportionate, and exorbitant."* All of these words simply mean that when a person displays this aspect of pride, they have an overinflated view of themselves. This is what a puffer fish does when it feels threatened; it inflates itself which causes poisonous spikes to protrude from its body. The poison is very toxic. Likewise, negative pride in a marriage is toxic to the harmony and longevity of that marriage. The person displaying the pride prevents their spouse from getting close. In other words, negative pride prevents intimate, open and honest communication between a husband and wife!

Now, lest you think I'm just speaking out of turn, I want to remind you that the Bible has a lot to say about pride. I chose the following scriptures on pride because I believe they apply to what we are learning about the effect of negative pride on a marriage.

Proverbs 11:2 (ESV) – When pride comes, then comes disgrace, but with the humble is wisdom.

Proverbs 13:10 (NLT) – Pride leads to conflict; those who take advice are wise.

Proverbs 16:18 (ESV) – Pride goes before destruction, and a haughty spirit before a fall.

Proverbs 18:12 (NIV) – Before his downfall a man's heart is proud, but humility comes before honor.

Proverbs 29:23 (ESV) – One's pride will bring him low, but he who is lowly in spirit will obtain honor.

Psalm 59:12 (NIV) – For the sins of their mouths, for the words of their lips, let them be caught in their pride.

1 Corinthians 13:4 (NIV) – Love is patient, love is kind. It does not envy, it does not boast, it is not proud.

As we look at the above scriptures collectively, two very important themes develop. First, negative pride in a marriage will dishonor your marriage. How? It causes disruption in the couple's communication because it breeds and/or causes arguments, and it destroys the intimacy of their relationship...it deals a harsh blow to the couple's cohesiveness and mutual trust because pride is divisive! A prideful husband or wife dishonors his or her marriage vows. It negates his or her vow to be "mutually submissive in reverence of Christ!" When a couple becomes victims of this type of pride, it will manifest itself as sins of our mouths and our lips...it is seen in the "verbal missiles" the couple starts lobbing back and forth at each other! They say things they later regret and they find themselves feeling guilty because they know their attitude and their behavior was wrong...it was sinful...I am speaking to believers!

The second theme we see from the scriptures above shows us the result of letting our pride go! Here is it! When we keep our pride in check, we will gain wisdom and honor. We gain wisdom because we listen and we learn. None of us have cornered the market on knowing everything... only God is omniscient...the rest of us know bits and pieces, regardless of how educated we are or how smart we think we are. And because none of us know everything, all of us can learn something from someone else. To understand this simple concept is the first step of wisdom...when I recognize that I don't know everything and can learn from others, I have just positioned myself to gain wisdom. The husband can learn from his wife and the wife can learn from her husband.

Now, here's the kicker! The wisdom we learn may not initially make us happy. Sometimes the wisdom we receive is feedback that points to our shortcomings or flaws...to the areas in our personal and/or spiritual life where we are challenged to grow. In either case, the wisdom we receive, though potentially painful at first sight or hearing, can propel us to grow in our marital as well as our spiritual relationships. Interestingly enough, for believers, these relationships are parallel because in both we are called to worship and honor God!

Speaking of honor, this is the main part of the second theme that rings true as a result of us removing pride from our marriage. I see honor as what the married couple gives to each other by obeying their last command from God's Word. Remember the wife's last command to respect her husband and the husband's last command to honor his wife as the weaker or "more delicate" vessel? Well simply put, a husband can't and won't honor his wife if he allows pride to rule him. Likewise, a wife can't and won't respect her husband if she allows pride to rule her. That brings us back again to God's very first collective command to both the husband and wife in Ephesians 5:21, *"submit yourselves to each other out of reverence for Christ."*

EFFECTIVE COMMUNICATION REQUIRES US TO UNDERSTAND OUR MATE

As a man and as a husband, I've heard other men say things like "women are hard to understand!" While this may be true to a certain extent, husbands let me let you in on a little, well-known secret; you don't really need to understand women…you only need to understand <u>one</u> woman…your wife! This same principle holds true for wives. I've overheard women, in speaking to other women about the difficulties of dealing with men, say they have to train their man like you would a dog. I must admit, it wasn't a pretty picture. In other words, their philosophy behind this idea is that you have to understand the *breed* of dog you have, so you can anticipate its behavior. Are you for real??? However, in retrospect, I can almost understand those women's ideologies because men have been known to act "doggish!" Sorry guys!!!!

What both sexes are saying is that we as men and women need to work hard and intentionally put forth great efforts to understand our mates… perhaps a stronger way to say this is that we need to get to *know* our husband or wife. The word *know* has the implication of having <u>intimate</u> knowledge of your mate...this is not just surface or general knowledge...rather, this is in-depth knowledge and understanding of your mate obtained by intentionally studying them! This is akin to what God has done for us. According to Jeremiah 1:5, God knew us before we were *"formed in our mother's womb"* and in Jeremiah 29:11, He *"knows the thoughts and the plans"* he has for us. We as husbands and wives must be <u>*intentional*</u> about getting to know our mate. This means that our efforts must be specifically focused on getting to know his or her needs; his or her goals; the way he or she receives love and shows love; and how he or she communicates, including how he or she receives criticism!

Our intentional efforts to understand our mate requires us to ask our mate questions designed to elicit a descriptive response...that is; we must ask questions that do not simply have a "yes" or "no" answer. Effective communication results from dialogue between the husband and wife. We must closely observe our mate and mentally record things about the way they communicate. Are there certain words or gestures that make your mate cringe or even verbally, mentally or emotionally shutdown? If so, you will need to find a way around those words or gestures to get your message across to your mate. We must be careful to avoid being verbally aggressive as well as being verbally condescending; both of these inhibit effective communication.

Dr. Paul C and Teri K Reisser, authors of *Your Spouse Isn't the Person You Married*, wrote an article that first appeared in the September/October, 2010 issue of the Thriving Family Magazine and was originally titled *"Get to Know Your Spouse ... All Over Again."* The following excerpts are from their article that was posted online and is now titled *"Who Did You Marry: Understanding Your Spouse."* The article speaks directly to the importance of us being intentional about not only understanding our spouse, but making this a continual process:

Your school days may be long behind you, but you never need to stop learning...Unfortunately, there is one subject that far too many adults stop learning about: the person they married. The natural drift in a marital relationship is to stop learning about the other person and to lose track of his or her thoughts and feelings…this occurs because after a couple gets married and settles into everyday life, the responsibilities of work, housekeeping, child care, family finances and other commitments often move those intimate, open conversations to the back burner.

This lack of continued intimacy and open communication, which results in the couple intentionally and continually learning about each other, is a detrimental blow to a marriage. The empty nest syndrome is a potential wake-up call to the couple as realization that after the last child has left the nest, they have nothing to talk about. The downfall comes when one or both secretly internalize that his or her need for those "intimate, learning more about each other" conversations between the couple haven't happened for months or even years, and the formerly close couple looks for fulfilment by someone else…the need for this verbal intimacy can and often does lead to extramarital physical intimacy that is usually first unintentional and highly regrettable.

http://www.thrivingfamily.com/Features/Magazine/2010/sep/who-did-you-marry-understanding-your-spouse.aspx

If you find your marriage with this problem, I recommend you read their entire online article and even more so, I highly recommend you invest in purchasing a copy of their book, *Your Spouse Isn't the Person You Married: Keeping Love Strong through Life's Changes.* My wife and I purchased the book and it is filled with insightful information and recommendations to help a couple regain their intimacy…it is a must read for married couples! For example, Chapter One of their book is entitled, *"Who's That Sleeping in My Bed?"* The chapter ends with an exercise, which is intended to help the couple find out just how well they know each other. Let me reiterate what I previously said; this is a must read for married couples!

EFFECTIVE COMMUNICATION REQUIRES US TO BE TIMELY

Before concluding this chapter on communication, it's imperative that I discuss one other issue that is related to, and absolutely necessary for effective communication in marriage. In order for communication to be effective, especially when discussing difficult issues, it must be timely!

The first aspect of timeliness deals with failing to discuss a difficult matter at the time an incident occurs or immediately thereafter. One of the worst things a husband or wife can do is to withhold discussing a matter with their mate, that has hurt them or caused them concern, and then bring it up for the first time six weeks later. By failing to discuss this matter in a timely manner or as soon as possible after an incident occurred, the one who withheld the information has caused undue stress on the relationship. It will often display itself in that person being short or irritable, apparently for no reason. This can and is often followed by hurtful words, a distant or passive-aggressive attitude, and especially a disruption in the intimacy of the marriage. It can lead their mate to begin wondering if there is some type of extra-marital activity going on. When this happens, the seeds of doubt and mistrust will have been planted, and if left unchecked, those seeds will grow into a massive tree of doubt and mistrust.

In fact, timely communication is God-ordained! The Bible tells us in Matthew 5:23-24 (NASB), *"Therefore if you are presenting your offering at the altar, and there remember that your brother has something against you, leave your offering there before the altar and go; first be reconciled to your brother, and then come and present your offering."* In other words, God does not want our worship, if we are not in right relationship with our fellow believer. In Proverbs 25:12 (NLT), the Bible tells us, *"Valid criticism is as treasured by the one who heeds it as jewelry made from the finest gold."* As believing husbands and wives, we owe it to each other to bring our hurts and concerns to our mate as soon as possible so the matter can be resolved. Remember, your mate cannot properly respond to and resolve a situation that he or she does not know about, and especially those things that happened in the distant past!

The second aspect of timeliness deals with choosing to push for a discussion of a truly trivial matter at an inconvenient time. This usually involves one wanting to have his or her way, and it reeks of selfishness! In several counseling sessions with married couples, I've often heard the wife complain about her husband not wanting to talk or that he is not a good communicator. The wife would say something like, "Two nights ago, I wanted to talk to him about something that happened at work and my husband couldn't stop watching the basketball game." Inevitably, the husband would respond with something like, "It wasn't just a basketball game; it was the NBA finals and my team was winning!"

What this really amounts to is this--the timeliness of effective communication depends on *the true need* to discuss a matter at a specific moment, even if it means interrupting something that is important to your husband or wife. My wife and I have made a practice of letting each other know if something we need to discuss is a "right now" issue or one that can wait a little bit later. If it can wait until later, that doesn't mean that we put off the issue to be discussed to some undetermined later time; we will let each other know the approximate time frame, i.e., with something like, "Can we talk about it in an hour, or as soon as this show is over?" It is the courteous, respectful, loving and right thing to do for both parties. It lets your mate know that you want to hear what they have to say, and their actions let you know that they value your time and your attention. In Proverbs 15:23 (NLT), the Bible tells us, *"Everyone enjoys a fitting reply; it is wonderful to say the right thing at the right time!"* What an awesome verse! All of us ought to remember this verse and apply it to our marriages, as well as other relationships!

One other aspect of timeliness deals with the absolutely bad timing of trying to insist on discussing a difficult matter at the wrong time, i.e., while in the presence of family or friends. This usually results in embarrassment to your mate and in the dismay of those around you. This usually occurs when either the husband or the wife shows no respect for his or her mate, or the disrespect is mutual. Perhaps an example is in order here to explain what I mean. Let's say a couple is at social event, such as a school reunion or an event in the neighborhood where one of them grew up. The husband or wife sees their mate talking to a person of the opposite sex whom he or she doesn't know and the other person *appears* to have more than a passing interest in their mate. The husband or wife decides to go over and break this up! He or she storms over and grabs his mate by the arm, dragging them away, and says rather loudly "I want to talk to you right now!"

Would we as the husband or wife be within our rights to go over and see what's going on or make ourselves known to the person talking to our mate? Yes, by all means! However, we may better serve our position and purpose, and also maintain our composure by observing our mate to see how he or she handles being approached by a person of the opposite sex. If the we observe the exchange and don't see our mate acting in an inappropriate manner, then we could simply walk over to them, and more than likely, our mate will immediately introduce us to the other person with something like, "Pam (or John), this is my lovely wife, Jodie (or handsome husband, Phillip), whom I was telling you about."

The other reason we as husbands or wives should be cautious about the way we walk over and aggressively insert ourselves into what we *think* may be a threatening situation, is because we don't know the content of the conversation between the other person and our mate. Wouldn't it be a shame if the other person had no romantic interest at all in our mate, but was only telling him or her that one of their professional colleagues had provided his or her resume to them? What if the person wanted to know if our mate was interested in a senior manager position at the corporation where they are the Vice-President of Human Resources? Wouldn't it be ironic if the smile we saw on the other person's face was their astonishment with the fact that they had just reviewed our mate's resume the day before, Friday, and had planned to call our mate on Monday...and he or she ran into our mate on Saturday at this event? What if other person's smile was a reflection of the joy they felt in believing that God had ordained their meeting with our mate at this event...at that specific time? And what if, we messed it all up because we were untimely and inappropriate with our actions? What if we caused our mate to lose out on a great opportunity simply because we decided to insist on inserting our right to discuss our feelings with our mate at that very moment? Hopefully, all of us with stop and think about how our untimely actions can erode our mate's reputation and even impact potential blessings that could benefit our families!

We close this chapter on the importance of a commitment to effective communication with a reminder that the failure to engage in quality, intentional communication can destroy our marriages. In fact, a Huffington Post online article reported the following:

> A group of 100 mental health professionals were polled to determine the most common problems found in dysfunctional marriages. The poll results indicated that the lack of effective communication (65%) in a marriage by far had the greatest impact on the marriage leading to a divorce. This was followed by the failure of couples to properly respond to and resolve conflict (43%).
>
> *http://www.huffingtonpost.com/2013/11/20/divorce-causes-_n_4304466.html*

The results of the aforementioned poll ought to be enough to make every couple strive for timely and effective communication. I have one last comment. Effective communication that is open and honest and recurring enhances the couple's emotional intimacy, which in turn enhances a couple's physical intimacy. That was just food for thought!

Chapter Nine Questions to Ponder and Discuss

1. What topics of concern to you do you find it the hardest to discuss with your husband or wife?

2. What are your biggest reasons for your apprehension in discussing those topics with your husband or wife?

3. If you're unequally yoked in your marriage, what are you doing to ensure that you remain faithful to God's commands in your communication with your spouse?

4. Which two scriptures related to how we should talk to our husband or wife as our brother or sister in Christ most affects you, and why?

5. Do you consider mutual respect to be common in your marriage; why or why not?

6. If you have experienced episodes of disrespect in your marriage, what have you done to remedy the problem; and if so, how successful have your remedies been?

7. What steps, if any, do you take to quell the rise of your pride when you are having a serious discussion/debate with your spouse?

8. Do you sometimes wonder if your spouse is the same person you initially married, if so, why?

Note: To help you with effective communication in your marriage as well as getting to really know or re-know each other, please go to the following websites for these free exercises:

http://www.soulsupportcounselingct.com/quiz/How-Well-Do-You-Know-Your-Partner-Quiz/

http://decisionquiz.com/articles/we-can-communicate-better-an-exercise-designed-to-give-couples-a-satisfying-experience-of-communicating/

http://ocw.usu.edu/Family__Consumer____Human_Development/Marriage___Family_Relationships/Communication__Conflict___Commitment_6.html

CHAPTER 10

Avoiding Satan's Pitfalls and Snares

*Submit yourselves therefore to God. Resist the devil, and he will
flee from you. Draw near to God, and he will draw near to you.*

— JAMES 4:7-8

EVERY MARRIAGE, AND ESPECIALLY THOSE of believers who are in a biblical
marriage, will face attacks from Satan. For some, it will seem constant. If
you find yourself in that group, I challenge you to first take a look at your
relationship with God and see through His Word if you are honoring Him
in your Christian walk. For others of us, we will experience times when
Satan tries to attack our marriages and then times of peaceful harmony
in our marriages. If your marriage is like this, then just know that those
times of peaceful harmony is simply Satan reloading his weapons and reas-
sessing how he can best attack your marriage the next time! Remember
from our discussion earlier in the book; Satan is attacking your marriage
simply because God ordained it!

Because we know that Satan hates what God has instituted and
ordained, we should always expect Satan to attack us in every aspect of
our lives; our biblical marriage is no different. In fact, we can see from the
times that we live in that biblical marriage is under unprecedented attacks
from every direction! I believe that Satan has unleashed a full, all-out war
against God's plan for marriage and family. It shows in the record number

of divorces, especially among those in the Church. We can see this very clearly in the *softening* and even collapse of the Church's stance on biblical marriage among several denominations that previously had unwavering views and morals regarding biblical marriage. Furthermore, some have even completely compromised with the world system on marriage and abandoned biblical tenets of marriage as an institution "between a man and a woman who become husband and wife," and have now accepted and even seemingly courting those in society who are involved in same-sex relationships and marriages.

So for us who choose to worship God in our marriage and remain true to His precepts, we must be committed to avoid Satan's pitfalls, schemes and traps, which he is constantly using to try to ensnare us. Satan's only purpose is to destroy our marriages and thus our testimonies for God! As we look at what we must do to uphold God's standards for marriage, we will be focusing on how Satan tries to attack us and our marriages, and how we can avoid becoming victims to his pitfalls.

Perhaps one of the biggest pitfalls of Satan, which we must absolutely strive to avoid, is that of defiling ourselves. Defilement has serious meanings; let's take a look at the definition of defilement.

Defilement - To make unclean; to render foul or dirty; to make impure; to render turbid; as, the water is defiled; to soil; to tarnish; as reputation; to pollute; to make ceremonially unclean; to corrupt chastity; to debauch; to violate; to tarnish the purity of character by lewdness; to taint, in a moral sense; to corrupt; to render impure with sin. (KJV Bible Dictionary)

When we look at this very comprehensive definition of defilement, a recurring theme should jump out at us. When we defile ourselves or allow others to defile us, we become morally and spiritually unclean...in other words, we dirty ourselves! It's like having a flock of Canadian geese fly over your previously clean pool and they fill it with their droppings. Do you get the picture now? Right; it's a disgusting mental picture...or for some of you, it may be something that you actually experienced. Now, we can all imagine how God feels when we defile ourselves while falling for Satan's pitfalls. Let's now look at two areas of potential defilement.

PERSONAL DEFILEMENT

I would like to begin with a picture that each of us should keep in our mind. It is a story of triumph for God, even when surrounded by the enemy like the world system in which we live, which is enmity against God. In Daniel 1, we can read the story of Daniel and his three friends who were taken away as captives from their home in Jerusalem and taken to Babylon. They found themselves in an environment where enjoying the pleasures of the flesh was rampant. Daniel and his friends were faced with a life-changing decision...to either eat the food that had been offered to idols, which would be a direct affront to God...or to make a radical decision to avoid these foods that would defile them! In Daniel 1:8 (NLT), we read of Daniel's bold decision which for me, is absolutely one of the most profound scriptures in the Bible, and one that for me is a *rhema* word by which I live: *"But Daniel made up his mind not to defile himself by eating the food and wine given to them by the king..."*

This is the mindset that each believer must have, first and foremost, in his or her relationship with God. You see, Satan doesn't usually start out by getting the couple to compromise; he starts with one of them, be it the husband or the wife! We all of course have heard or read in 1 Peter 5:8 that Satan is like a roaring lion seeking whom he may destroy. Then, we must know that he is out to take us down...to make us fall...to cause us to defile ourselves! In 1 Corinthians 3:16-17 (KJV) we read, *"Know ye not that ye are the temple of God, and that the Spirit of God dwelleth in you? If any man defile the temple of God, him shall God destroy; for the temple of God is holy, which temple ye are."*

Since we know that Satan is like a roaring lion seeking to destroy us, what must we do to avoid his pitfalls? The answer is found in the following verse, 1 Peter 5:8-9 (KJV), *"Be sober, be vigilant; because your adversary the devil, as a roaring lion, walketh about, seeking whom he may devour: Whom resist in the faith, knowing that the same afflictions are accomplished in your brethren that are in the world."* There are three things we must do according to this scripture.

First, we must remain *sober*; that means we must be self-disciplined in order to refrain from acting out on the desires of our flesh. In other words, we must not allow our flesh to control how we respond to temptations of the mind and the body! To remain sober implies that we are not like a person under the influence and control of alcohol or chemical substances... those who cannot control their actions and instead act out and do things they would not normally do.

When we don't remain sober, we will do things according to the lusts of our own flesh, and then we have the audacity to say, "...the devil made me do it!" No, Satan didn't make you do it; you did it because you wanted to do it! Satan doesn't have power over us, unless we give it to him! Another verse that guides my spiritual walk and compels me to remain sober is the inspired words Paul wrote in Titus 2:11-12 (KJV), *"For the grace of God that bringeth salvation hath appeared to all men, Teaching us that, denying ungodliness and worldly lusts, we should live soberly, righteously, and godly, in this present world."* We must live sober, Spirit-controlled lives!

Secondly, we must be *vigilant*! This does not mean that we are just standing around watching and waiting for Satan to attack and then we respond. This means being proactive and always on alert! Jesus spoke of this kind of alertness in Matthew 26:40-41 (KJV) in His words to Peter, James and John: *"And he cometh unto the disciples, and findeth them asleep, and saith unto Peter, What, could ye not watch with me one hour? Watch and pray, that ye enter not into temptation: the spirit indeed is willing, but the flesh is weak."* It is like the alertness of an Army patrol that is on a scout mission to find the enemy and sound the warning before the enemy can get close enough to do any damage or launch a surprise attack against the main force. The scout patrol takes an assessment of the enemy's position, numbers, weapons and any potential traps and then notifies the main force on what they need to do to defeat the enemy. Just like this Army patrol, we must remain alert for Satan who is on the prowl...in other words, he is trying to sneak up on us and attack any spot we leave unprotected! Let's stay alert!

This is a great place to include a biblical picture of Satan's activities to seduce us to fall for his trap. Look at the following scripture from Proverbs 7:1-27 (NLT):

[1]Follow my advice, my son; always treasure my commands. [2]Obey them and live! Guard my teachings as your most precious possession. [3]Tie them on your fingers as a reminder. Write them deep within your heart. [4]Love wisdom like a sister; make insight a beloved member of your family. [5]Let them hold you back from an affair with an immoral woman, from listening to the flattery of an adulterous woman.

[6]I was looking out the window of my house one day [7]and saw a simpleminded young man who lacked common sense. [8]He was crossing the street near the house of an immoral woman. He was strolling down the path by her house [9]at twilight, as the day was fading, as the dark of night set in. [10]The woman approached him, dressed seductively and sly of heart. [11]She was the brash, rebellious type who never stays at home. [12]She is often seen in the streets and markets, soliciting at every corner. [13]She threw her arms around him and kissed him, and with a brazen look she said, [14]"I've offered my sacrifices and just finished my vows. [15]It's you I was looking for! I came out to find you, and here you are! [16]My bed is spread with colored sheets of finest linen imported from Egypt. [17]I've perfumed my bed with myrrh, aloes, and cinnamon. [18]Come, let's drink our fill of love until morning. Let's enjoy each other's caresses, [19]for my husband is not home. He's away on a long trip. [20]He has taken a wallet full of money with him, and he won't return until later in the month." [21]So she seduced him with her

pretty speech. With her flattery she enticed him. ²²He followed her at once, like an ox going to the slaughter or like a trapped stag, ²³awaiting the arrow that would pierce its heart. He was like a bird flying into a snare, little knowing it would cost him his life.

²⁴Listen to me, my sons, and pay attention to my words. ²⁵Don't let your hearts stray away toward her. Don't wander down her wayward path. ²⁶For she has been the ruin of many; numerous men have been her victims. ²⁷Her house is the road to the grave. Her bedroom is the den of death.

Although this scripture is speaking to men, it also easily applies to women. We all know that there are slick-talking men out there who only have one thing on their mind...to seduce a woman they perceive as vulnerable. When I was in the Air Force and stationed in Germany, there was an American guy whose wife was also in the Air Force. I remember one day that a single Air Force mother arrived in Germany. I overheard the guy tell her to let him know if she needed anything, and that he could help her financially if she needed. I asked him about what he had said to this woman. He said it was all for the purpose of getting in her pants. I know that sound callous, but that was his purpose in offering his help to her. There was no chivalry involved...only selfish, lustful intentions on his part, which he proudly admitted!

Does this seem unreal? It shouldn't because there are women all around us who are settling for "help" without realizing the strings...no, the "chains" that are attached to that help! Wives, there are men who look for women who seem to be having marital trouble...they overhear you on the phone having an argument with your husband while you're on your lunch break at work...they watch your demeanor when you are leaving work to go home...and then they began to scheme and plan how they will take advantage of the situation! Just as Solomon wrote for the men not to become prey to the adulterous woman, women you must not become prey to the adulterous man.

I started to move away from this, but the Holy Spirit brought me back to include a specific warning for our sisters in Christ. Here it is: Don't become a "silly or gullible woman!" This is what the Apostle Paul writes to Timothy when warning him to watch out for false teachers who will try to take advantage of those in the church, especially the women who were gullible. Look at what Paul said in in 2 Timothy 3:6 (NKJV): *"For of this sort are those who creep into households and make captives of gullible women loaded down with sins, led away by various lusts."* Petersen in his MSG Bible said, *"These are the kind of people who smooth-talk themselves into the homes of unstable and needy women and take advantage of them..."* To my sisters in Christ, I urge you to be aware of "these men," and now, you must even be aware of "these women" who are truly wolves in sheep's clothing and they are on the prowl for those who they see as silly, gullible, unstable and needy! If you're rooted and grounded in the Lord, then those words don't describe you! Okay, I'm moving on!

As believers, we must take a stand and commit to not defile ourselves. When Satan comes with his temptations, and he surely will, we must remember to stand on God's Word. We can never become over confident and allow ourselves to get into potentially compromising situations...we must avoid tempting environments, people, and activities! Paul said it like this in 1 Corinthians 10:12 (ESV), *"12 Therefore let anyone who thinks that he stands take heed lest he fall."*

MARITAL DEFILEMENT

Let me start by saying that where a marriage has been defiled, everyone involved loses! That includes the husband and wife, any kids, and any extended family. Extreme or repeated marital defilement can have generational consequences that extend to a couple's grandchildren, great-grandchildren and beyond. This is why Satan and his demonic forces are working overtime to defile marriages, especially among those in the Church. Satan does not care whether you are a pastor, deacon, ministry leader, missionary, or a lay member; he is only concerned with creating opportunities for us to defile our marriages. The Bible tells us in Hebrews 13:4 (KJV), *"Marriage is honourable in all, and the bed undefiled: but whoremongers and adulterers God will judge."* This scripture makes it very clear regarding God's view of marital defilement. So, let's look at some ways we can defile our marriage.

Marital Infidelity

The most common way marriages are defiled is simply through marital infidelity or adultery. We hold no pretense here; this is when a husband or wife steps outside of their marriage and engage in a physical, sexual relationship with someone other than their spouse. Let me just add this...just in case you are thinking of only doing what former President Bill Clinton did with Monica Lewinski, know this...sexual touching, kissing, etc., is included in this marital defilement of infidelity! In fact, Jesus said in Matthew 5:28 (ESV): *"But I say to you that everyone who looks as a woman with lustful intent has already committed adultery with her in his heart."*

Marital infidelity often occurs due to inappropriate friendships with members of the opposite sex, or hanging out at places where the likelihood of this occurring in increased, like a night club. This also often occurs in inappropriate professional relationships with a coworker or even supervisor, which usually spills over to unintentional, one-night stands while on a business trip or some other office-related function. In fact, some office environments are a perfect breeding ground for extra-marital affairs—for example, success-driven, recognition-driven business environments are a perfect hunting ground for Satan in his role as a "roaring lion." Celebrations of major accomplishments can evolve into something more when we allow ourselves to celebrate like the world, where alcohol is the catalyst for having a great time!!! This is why it is absolutely critical for us as believing spouses to do what the Bible tells us in 1 Thessalonians 5:22 (KJV), *"Abstain from all appearance of evil."* In this verse, *abstain* means to refrain from, and *evil* means sin or wickedness. This verse clearly tells us that we must refrain from any and all events that have any resemblance to sin. So, a business meeting between you and your single manager at his or her apartment would certainly have the appearance of sin or wickedness. Don't do it! Am I overdoing it with this…I don't think so!

Inappropriate social relationships with individuals of the opposite sex are also highly successful hunting grounds for Satan. Husbands and wives, let's get one thing absolutely clear! You cannot hang-out with someone of the opposite sex on a continual, alone basis and think you won't begin to think impure thoughts! Let's face it; we live in a time of sexuality overload, and the sliminess of taboo lust will find us if we're not careful! Extensive time spent with former classmates, former neighborhood friends, gym acquaintances, etc., of the opposite sex and especially those who are not sold out for Christ, will more than likely result in a husband or wife as a minimum, committing adultery in his or her heart. And if the lustful thoughts get into our heart, Satan, acting as our personal sin valet, will serve you up one of his seemingly tasty, but toxic dishes! You might even find yourself fondly thinking of the lyrics of Luther Vandross's song, "If Only for One Night":

Let me hold you tight, if only for one night.
Let me keep you near, to ease away your fear,
It would be so nice, if only for one night.
I won't tell a soul, no one has to know,
If you want to be, totally discreet,
I'll be at your side, if only for one night.

Your eyes say things I never hear from you,
And my knees are shaking too,
But I'm willing to go thru.

I must be crazy standing in this place,
But I'm feeling no disgrace, for asking…
Let me hold you tight, if only for one night!

For many of us, that song brings back memories. So, are any of us so naïve as to think that we can handle being in the aforementioned types of environments and our flesh won't rise up? Look at themes that jump out from the lyrics above..."let me hold you tight for just one night;" "I won't tell anyone, we can be discreet;" "this will be our little secret;" "I know this is scary for you, but it's scary for me too, and yet, I feel no disgrace for wanting you!"

Ladies and gentlemen, we cannot allow ourselves to be tricked by the enemy. We all remember the story of King David and Bathsheba...in 2 Samuel 11, David hooked up with Bathsheba for just one night...I believe all the themes in the song above were present in the events of that evening...but the consequences followed David for the rest of his life! David had failed to obey God's command from Leviticus 18:20 (KJV), *"Moreover thou shalt not lie carnally with thy neighbour's wife, to defile thyself with her."* David absolutely defiled Bathsheba...and he defiled himself! Perhaps he preyed on her loneliness since her husband was away for an extended period fighting for Israel against their enemies. We must be watchful for anything that seems to be pushing us to commit any sin, especially a grievous sin such as adultery that has far-reaching implications! In Genesis 39:9, Joseph called adultery a *"great wickedness and sin."*

Let's look at a scripture that although it speaks to men, it is equally applicable to women...so husbands and wives take note. In Proverbs 6:24-29 (NLT) we read the following:

> [24] It will keep you from the immoral woman, from the smooth tongue of a promiscuous woman. [25] Don't lust for her beauty. Don't let her coy glances seduce you. [26] For a prostitute will bring you to poverty, but sleeping with another man's wife will cost you your life. [27] Can a man scoop a flame into his lap and not have his clothes catch on fire? [28] Can he walk on hot coals and not blister his feet? [29] So it is with the man who sleeps with another man's wife. He who embraces her will not go unpunished.

Verses 27 and 28 are pivotal verses that every believing husband and wife must ponder. Can we really play with fire and not get burnt? Most times, we think we can control the fire because we started it. However, when the wind gets hold of a fire, it will send the fire careening out of control and it becomes a wildfire. When I was stationed in South Korea, one day I was trying to light my grill using a piece of rolled-up newspaper. I lit the newspaper and was lighting the grill when the wind blew embers from the newspaper onto the grass. Before I knew it, the fire had spread. It took firemen from the local Korean fire station as well as some from the Air Base to put out the fire. It was embarrassing. I made the newspaper...but that wasn't how I wanted to be known.

Husband and wives, you can be sure that all Satan is doing is standing by waiting for us to start a fire...a little flirting here or there...a well-placed look or compliment...you know, something like this..."*I don't mean to be disrespectful, but I can tell you have been working out and losing weight because you look gorgeous in that dress; wow!*" Or, "*I can tell you've been working out because the way you look in that muscle shirt, umm, Morris Chestnut or Bradley Cooper ain't got nothing on you!*" That's all Satan was waiting for... you lit the fire; now he will blow it out of control and consume you! And then your name will be floating around on Facebook, Twitter and other social media in a way that I'm sure you didn't want it to be!

Proverbs 6:24-25 from the scripture above reminds us to keep away from immoral people and their smooth tongues...their smooth words are like a snake slithering toward you ready to sink its sharp, poison-laced fangs into your hand...or like a python waiting to squeeze the life out of you! We must be careful not to fall into lust because "she looks good" or "he looks good." We must not let their flirting looks cause us to lower our guard. Remember, Satan is just waiting for the first spark...and then he will do his best to cause a wildfire. And when that happens, what you thought you could keep under wraps now becomes front-page news. Perhaps you think I am just saying this. In Luke 8:17 (NLT), Jesus said, "*For all that is secret will eventually be brought into the open, and everything that is concealed will be brought to light and made known to all.*" Just like God didn't allow

David's sin to remain hidden, we can expect that ours won't remain hidden! So we must ask ourselves this question: Is one night of fleshly passion worth a lifetime of sorrow and regrets, broken homes and lives, and curses to the third and fourth generations? For me, the answer is a definite "No!"

MARITAL SWINGING

One of the other forms of marital defilement is when both the husband and wife are complicit in that great wickedness and sin against God. I speak of none other than couples who get involving in "swinging" wherein they engage in supposedly unemotional, sexual orgies with other couples. I know that almost all of you reading this book won't believe this is happening among those who attend Christian churches across America, but I can assure you that it happens and is happening! In fact, it happened with at least two couples at a church I used to attend. Once it became known, the church leadership exercised biblical church discipline. It caused division in the church because one of the husbands was an elder at the church. Yes, you heard me right…he was an elder! But remember we have already established that Satan does not care what your position is in the church; his only concern is whether or not he can cause you to fall!

If you don't think this is a problem among those who call themselves Christians, all you need to do is look at the website called "Liberated Christians." Their online article entitled "Swingers – Happy, Safe, Healthy, Well Adjusted, Mainstream Americans," said:

> Up to 90% of swingers identify with a religion and up to 47% regularly attend their place of worship (Friendship Express 1994 & Miller 1994). Although sexual promiscuity is posited as the antithesis of emotional fidelity in the western romantic tradition, swingers maintain that joint experiences of recreational sex enhance their sexual and emotional bonds. By openly acknowledging their individual desires for sexual variety and pursuing these needs together, swingers claim to obviate the usual sources

of deceit, betrayal and guilt in relationships. These destructive impulses, they say, are replaced with a deeper understanding and a higher plane of trust. Some have argued that because of the very high degree of mutual knowledge and trust, this mental bond displaces sex from its status dictated by Judeo-Christian tradition as the central mystery of a relationship.

http://www.libchrist.com/swing/happysafestudies.html

Wow…can you believe that? One of the issues in swinging is that couples who call themselves Christians, have to ultimately rationalize or find an acceptable excuse for their actions to the point that they can see their actions as not violating God's Word. They make excuses for their actions and even try to say that swinging helps them have a better marriage that honors God's command that what He has put together, let no man tear apart (Mark 10:9). Are they for real????

They further rationalize their actions to the point that they violate one part of God's Word in order to supposedly obey another part of His Word…in reality, their supposed obedience to God is self-gratifying, self-serving and is about their own pleasure! Paul dealt with this very same thing among those who wanted to be a part of the early Church, but who at the same time held Gnostic views. The Gnostics believed that the body and spirit were separate and that what they did with their body was separate from what they did in their spirit. One of Paul's responses to this issue is found in Romans 12:1-2 (ESV), *"I appeal to you therefore, brothers, by the mercies of God, to present your bodies as a living sacrifice, holy and acceptable to God, which is your spiritual worship. Do not be conformed to this world, but be transformed by the renewal of your mind, that by testing you may discern what is the will of God, what is good and acceptable and perfect."*

This scripture requires believers to be intentional and specific in our worship to God. Therefore, couples who choose to swing and call themselves Christians are simply disobedient to God and out of his will, and there are no "ifs, ands or buts" about this! What makes this even worse is that they know it, but they continue their swinging activities because they have allowed themselves to become numb to the leading of the Holy Spirit...thus, they "grieve the Holy Spirit" (Ephesians 4:30).

To really drive home my point above, consider the following excerpt from "Swingers in Love: A Case for Christian Swinging," from an online blog at http://swingers-in-love.blogspot.com/p/case-for-christian-swinging.html. <u>Note</u>: Where there are *italicized* words inside of word brackets (*[]*), I have placed there for emphasis. I initially planned to insert this excerpt for emphasis on this pitfall, but then the Holy Spirit prompted me to comment on it. I have also placed my response to the blog's anonymous author preceded by "My Comments":

> Between the two swinging capitols of Las Vegas and Denver is a large religious community that promotes virtue, family and fidelity. At first blush, this community may appear antithetical to the swinging lifestyle, but as one who has bridged this gap, I can provide insight to *[how a couple can be both a faithful Christian and an active swinger.]*
>
>> <u>My Comments</u>: The author indicates that a supposedly Christian couple can be both *faithful* Christians and active swingers. Her reasoning is extremely flawed. First of all, when we look at the meaning of faith in the Greek (G4102) using Vine's Concise Dictionary of the Bible, we find information about faith that the author certainly appears to lack — "The main elements in *faith* in its relation to the invisible God, are (1) a firm conviction, producing a full acknowledgement of God's revelation or truth; (2) a personal surrender to Him; and (3) a conduct inspired by such surrender." A faithful Christian is one who strives to follow what Christ said in Mark 8:34 (KJV), "*Whosoever will come after me, let him deny himself, and take up his cross, and follow me.*" Throughout this blog, the author has shown that for

sure, her and her husband have not fully acknowledged the truth of God's Word; they have not surrendered their lives to Him to the point that He is their Lord; and they have yet to deny themselves which would lead them to display conduct showing a surrendered life! Instead, the author's words indicate that she and her husband are following a philosophy of man and not the Word of God!

Both communities have things in common. They place a high value on marriage, and family life. *[Sixty-seven percent of swingers say that it's possible to love both swinging and Jesus, almost half regularly attend religious services, and more than half say they are very religious.]*

My Comments: The blog's author again demonstrates either her ignorance of God's Word or her rejection of His Word. It is impossible to love both swinging and Jesus! Jesus said in John 14:15 (KJV), *"If ye love me, keep my commandments."* The author and her husband's love of swinging are evident that they love this world system, which is encompassed in their lust of the flesh, which has no connection with God. The Apostle John addressed this issue as recorded in 1 John 2:15-16 (NKJV), *"Do not love the world or the things in the world. If anyone loves the world, the love of the Father is not in him. For all that is in the world-- the lust of the flesh, the lust of the eyes, and the pride of life-- is not of the Father but is of the world."*

The blog author's comments about the swingers who attend church services and say they are religious, doesn't amount to a "hill of beans." I'm glad she at least noted they "attend" church instead of saying they are "in" the Church. As believers, we explicitly recognize that everyone who enters a church building is not in the *ecclesia* or the Church which Jesus spoke of in Matthew 16:18 (KJV) when He told Peter, *"upon this rock I will build my church; and the gates of hell shall not prevail against it."* There are many people who attend church in order to be identified with Christianity or out of a sense of duty. Jesus exposed those types of people in Matthew 15:7-9 (ESV), *"You hypocrites! Well did Isaiah prophesy of you, when he said: 'This people honors me with their lips, but their heart is far from me; in vain do they worship me, teaching as doctrines the commandments of men."* There will be a very, very sad ending for these types of people, if they die in their sins having rejected a true relationship where Jesus is not only their Savior, but also their Lord and Master. Jesus said in Matthew 7:21-23 (KJV), *"Not every one that saith unto me, Lord, Lord, shall enter into the kingdom of heaven; but he that doeth the will of my Father which is in heaven. Many will say to me in that day, Lord, Lord, have we not prophesied in thy name? and in thy name have cast out devils? and in thy name done many wonderful works? And then will I profess unto them, I never knew you: depart from me, ye that work iniquity."*

My husband and I were both raised in a very conservative upper-class religious community. We've been married for many years, have children, and *[we actively serve in church.]* Because of this, we keep our swinging activities discrete—*[not because we can't reconcile our actions]*, but because we think that our friends and family could not, and we chose to not have to explain ourselves.

My comments: The blog's author's confusion now becomes starkly clear. She apparently believes that actively serving in church negates their sinful, extra-marital activities. Is she hoping that her and her husband's good deeds will outweigh their sins? The Bible tells us in Romans 6:23 (NKJV), *"For the wages of sin is death, but the gift of God is eternal life in Christ Jesus our Lord."* The Bible does not offer an alternative plan of salvation based on "good deeds" or serving in church. Can we usher enough or greet visitors enough to earn our way into heaven…or can we visit the sick enough or clean the church enough to have our sins forgiven and thus earn our way into heaven? Absolutely not!

The author also said that they have reconciled their actions and keep their swinging discreet, not because it bothers them or their conscience, but because they don't want to have to explain it to their family or friends. To the author, I would tell her that her worry of explaining their swinging to their family and friends shows that she values how they will feel more than she values what God thinks! It's not their family or friends that they will one day face in judgment; it will be the Almighty God and Judge who they must face. The Bible tells us in 2 Corinthians 5:10 (KJV), *"For we must all appear before the judgment seat of Christ; that every one may receive the things done in his body, according to that he hath done, whether it be good or bad."* Their personal reconciliation of their swinging activities will have no bearing before the righteous standards of God!

And we're not the only ones. When looking at online classified ads soliciting swinging couples, relative to other areas in the US, the intermountain west has a huge number of ads that offer or solicit religious swingers. *[While some of these swingers may no longer live their religion, there are many such as ourselves who are active church attendees who practice their religion and maintain genuine belief. They, like us, reconcile their swinging activities with their religious beliefs.]*

<u>My comments</u>: This blog's author makes me wonder about just what are her genuine beliefs. Is she saying that she and her husband believe in Jesus? If so, that's not saying much as many in Jesus' day believed on Him, but still rejected Him. They saw and accepted His miracles and heard His teachings, but yet walked away from Him as their only way of salvation! Furthermore, for this author, her frail belief on Jesus only puts her on the same plain with the Satan's demons who also believe on Jesus. The Bible tells us in James 2:19 (ESV), *"You believe that God is one; you do well. Even the demons believe—and shudder!"* I like the way Eugene Petersen paraphrased this verse in the MSG Bible--*"Do I hear you professing to believe in the one and only God, but then observe you complacently sitting back as if you had done something wonderful? That's just great. Demons do that, but what good does it do them?"*

It also appears that the author was rallying others around her who believe the same way she and her husband believe—they have reconciled their swinging activities with their religious beliefs. Well, I can tell you that for me, there is nothing in what she has written that will convince me to reconcile their actions with what I know to directly violate God's Word. One verse, Hebrews 13:4 (ESV), says it all for me; *"Let marriage be held in honor among all, and let the marriage bed be undefiled, for God will judge the sexually immoral and adulterous."*

[When we started swinging, we did so for the same reasons that most people do: sexual thrill, adventure, etc.] However, there are additional reasons why we continue. Prior to marriage, we were both virgins, so eventually we developed a curiosity about having sex with others. Because, neither of us had the types of

sexual experiences that most people talk about, it was appealing to think that we might be able to experience a different sexual partner in a mutually agreed upon environment. *[Because conservative Christians have less sexual-dating experience prior to marriage, they see swinging as a way to explore the sexual-dating scene that they missed as youth.]* Once married and then permitted to have sex with each other, we later considered swinging as a way to engage in additional sexual exploration that we didn't have before marriage. *[Since both of us are consenting and participating in the activity, it makes our activities permissible. Religious teachings about sexuality address sex prior to marriage and fidelity within marriage, but do not forbid swinging.]*

<u>My comments</u>: I apologize, but I'm still laughing with dismay at the last italicized part of the preceding paragraph. Are we as believers to think that if two of us consent to participate in a sin, that makes it okay? For just a moment, let's move away from this author's fetish with adultery, although she gives it a seemingly less sinful name of swinging, since the word swinging is actually not found in the Bible. Okay, so the Bible tells us not to steal, kill, commit adultery, etc.; you all know the Ten Commandments. Based on the statement of this blog's author, if both my wife and I consent to cheating on our taxes and thus steal from the government, that makes our stealing permissible. I don't think that would go over very well with the Internal Revenue Service! And, I absolutely reject this author's assertion that because both her and her husband consented to participate in this act of adultery...oops, I meant swinging, that makes it permissible.

Perhaps this author should have read the story of Ananias and Sapphire in Acts 5:1-11; they consented and participated in a sin to lie to the Holy Ghost and it cost them their very lives. God didn't say, "Since they both consented to participate in this lie, I'll let them off the hook even though they violated my holy law." No, Ananias died first after he lied and his wife came along a little later and told the same lie...and she died too!

I'm not sure of which religious teachings about sexuality this author was referring to when she said they (those religious teachings) do not forbid swinging. However, I am absolutely certain the Bible forbids swinging...trying to perpetuate an otherwise lie because the word swinging does not appear in the Bible is simply a delusion of the devil! The Bible doesn't explicitly tell us not to use our phones for sexting...for those of you who are older like me, that refers to sending text messages that are raunchy or sexual in nature, and which could include photos of a sexual nature. However, the Bible does tell us in 1 Thessalonians 5:22 that we should avoid every activity that has the appearance of sin. Here's the question, would we feel good sending such a text to God? So, does the Bible really forbid swinging? Yes, swinging falls under adultery as well as sexual immorality in all of its forms. Look at the following scriptures:

1 Corinthians 6:9 (ESV) - Or do you not know that the unrighteous will not inherit the kingdom of God? Do not be deceived: neither the sexually immoral, nor idolaters, nor adulterers, nor men who practice homosexuality.

Ephesians 5:3-5 (ESV) - 3 But sexual immorality and all impurity or covetousness must not even be named among you, as is proper among saints. 4 Let there be no filthiness nor foolish talk nor crude joking, which are out of place, but instead let there be thanksgiving. [5] For you may be sure of this, that everyone who is sexually immoral or impure, or who is covetous (that is, an idolater), has no inheritance in the kingdom of Christ and God.

1 Thessalonians 4:3-5 (ESV)⁻ [3] For this is the will of God, your sanctification: that you abstain from sexual immorality; [4] that each one of you know how to control his own body in holiness and honor, [5] not in the passion of lust like the Gentiles who do not know God.

[Another attraction for the religious is that because swinging is a predominantly female-driven activity, it provides leadership for women, which is in contrast to predominantly male-lead religions. Swinging gives wives the ability to have more control in their marriage and to take the lead in social situations.]

<u>My comments</u>: It seems that the author has made the leap of swinging being more than just about them fulfilling their sexual fantasies; it now seems to be a part of their religious practices. King Solomon was right; there is nothing new under the sun. What the author describes is essentially reminiscent of ancient pagan worship involving sexual orgies. In those pagan religious practices, women were often priestesses. During the religious orgies, women controlled the flow of sexual activities, often having sex with numerous men in one night. Is this what this author is referring to? Or, is it a situation where she and her fellow female swingers have an issue with God's placement of the husband in the position as the head of the marriage and family? I suspect this author either doesn't really know God's plan for marriage, or she hasn't embraced it! We can

be absolutely sure that she certainly has disobeyed God's standard for holy living!

Additional attractions include its relationship to the biblical practice of polygamy, its admonishments to remain "Safe, Sane, and Sober", and "Don't Cheat. Swing." *[A careful study of scripture may cause a Christian to discover the difference between adultery (which is forbidden) and swinging (which is not).]*

> My comments: Say what? What version of the Bible did this author read to come up with this nonsense...admonishments to remain safe, sane, and sober, and don't cheat? I believe this author's first real issue is that she and her husband have not done a careful study of God's Word...I was intentional here with the use of God's Word because I'm not sure of what this author refers to when she uses the word "scripture." If they had searched out God's Word, then there is no way she can make such a farfetched statement!

If done slowly and with complete regard for the spouse's feelings, swinging can strengthen marriage by allowing couples to talk openly and honestly about their desires. *[If done to strengthen one's marriage, the religious can rightfully say that swinging falls within the spirit of the law and that the letter of the law does not specifically forbid this type of consensual sexual activity.]*

> My comments: Our very confused author must not have read Jesus' extensive discourse with the Samaritan woman as recorded in 4:1-24. If swinging truly does fall within the "spirit of the law," why would Jesus have brought up the woman's lifestyle and the fact that she was living in sin with a man that was not her husband?

Jesus obviously and intentionally pointed out her sin of sexual immorality. If our author is going to mention the spirit of the law, she ought to concentrate on what Jesus said in John 4:23-24 (ESV), *"But the hour is coming, and is now here, when the true worshipers will worship the Father in spirit and truth, for the Father is seeking such people to worship him. God is spirit, and those who worship him must worship in spirit and truth."*

Therefore, I'm not sure of what spirit she is referring to. I can only conclude that the author and her husband did indeed test the spirit by the spirit, and her spirit of wicked-desire connected with the wicked spirit waiting to fulfill her sinful desires. There is no indication of her checking with the Holy Spirit...at all!

While I understand that not everyone would agree with these interpretations, *[I have within myself been convinced of the harmony that can exist between one's religious belief and one's swinging practices. I do not need to forsake either one.]*

My comments: As I came to the end of this blog, I wondered how I would respond to this author's closing comment that she is convinced that her religious beliefs and swinging activities are in harmony. At last, I clearly see this author and her husband's true problem. They are religious, but they evidently lack a personal relationship with Jesus Christ! Their religion is impure, and therefore they are comfortable with defiling themselves. We read in James 1:27, *"Pure religion and undefiled before God and the Father is this, to visit the fatherless and widows in their affliction, and to keep oneself unspotted from the world."*

Although our author doesn't mention any of the specific activities involved in swinging, it is almost inevitable that some swinging activities will eventually bleed over to same-sex, sexual contact. As I considered this tidbit, the Holy Spirit gave me the scripture to put this all to rest. I close my comments on this author's blog with a text from Romans 1:18-32 (NLT). As you read this text, pay especially close attention to verses 24-32:

[18] But God shows "his anger from heaven against all sinful, wicked people who suppress the truth by their wickedness. [19] They know the truth about God because he has made it obvious to them. [20] For ever since the world was created, people have seen the earth and sky. Through everything God made, they can clearly see his invisible qualities—his eternal power and divine nature. So they have no excuse for not knowing God. [21] Yes, they knew God, but they wouldn't worship him as God or even give him thanks. And they began to think up foolish ideas of what God was like. As a result, their minds became dark and confused. [22] Claiming to be wise, they instead became utter fools. [23] And instead of worshiping the glorious, ever-living God, they worshiped idols made to look like mere people and birds and animals and reptiles.

[24] So God abandoned them to do whatever shameful things their hearts desired. As a result, they did vile and degrading things with each other's bodies. [25] They traded the truth about God for a lie. So they worshiped and served the things God created instead of the Creator himself, who is worthy of eternal praise! Amen. [26] That is why God abandoned them to their shameful desires. Even

the women turned against the natural way to have sex and instead indulged in sex with each other. [27] And the men, instead of having normal sexual relations with women, burned with lust for each other. Men did shameful things with other men, and as a result of this sin, they suffered within themselves the penalty they deserved. [28] Since they thought it foolish to acknowledge God, he abandoned them to their foolish thinking and let them do things that should never be done. [29] Their lives became full of every kind of wickedness, sin, greed, hate, envy, murder, quarreling, deception, malicious behavior, and gossip. [30] They are backstabbers, haters of God, insolent, proud, and boastful. They invent new ways of sinning, and they disobey their parents. [31] They refuse to understand, break their promises, are heartless, and have no mercy. [32] They know God's justice requires that those who do these things deserve to die, yet they do them anyway. Worse yet, they encourage others to do them, too.

A woman that my wife and I know shared with us a sad turn of events involving two couples who decided to swing together. These two couples began their swinging thinking that their individual marriages would not be affected. Well, ultimately their swinging led to each of the couples getting divorced. To make matters worse, they then married each other's former spouse. Can you imagine the baggage they brought into their new marriages? How can the couples in these newly formed marriages face each other knowing how their new marriages came about? For sure, trust will be an issue for these couples for a very long time, whether or not that trust issue is ever verbalized!

My brothers and sisters in Christ and fellow believing spouses, I don't know why the Holy Spirit put this issue of swinging on my heart, but I do know I felt compelled to include it here. I believe it was placed here to help someone, perhaps one of you who even at this moment is struggling with the desire to participate in this sexual sin...or perhaps you know someone who is participating in this sexual sin and you have felt compelled to lovingly confront them about their sin. I am absolutely sure that God had a reason for me to include this in this book, because it was never my intention to do so.

PORNOGRAPHY

One other pitfall of Satan we all must avoid is the introduction of pornography, in any form, into our marriages and homes. Most of us will never allow ourselves to be involved in actual swinging activities or physical adultery; and Satan knows that. So he will offer us a seemingly less scandalous alternative, something we can participate in at home without having to involve ourselves with other couples or individuals. Satan likes this alternative for us because he knows that many times we stay away from sin because we worry about others finding out. Satan knows that we can be absolutely discrete with this activity...he knows we can order it online and have it delivered to our homes in non-descript packages...and our neighbors, especially those who attend the same church we attend, would not know the difference even if they see us getting the package out of the mailbox or it being delivered by Fedex or UPS.

This particular pitfall is almost as addictive as if one became addicted to a chemical substance such as crack-cocaine. This is another area where a couple must rationalize their actions. One of the tricks of Satan is to have a couple believe that this will help them enhance their sexual intimacy. However, this idea has serious flaws. Although it may temporarily enhance a couple's sexual intimacy, the more permanent damage to the marital relationship comes from the introduction of others, albeit their image only, into the marriage. The human mind is like a DVD recorder; once the eyes see it, the mind can reproduce it with stark clarity over and over and over again. The result is that the wife will be wondering if her husband is thinking of her...or the woman in the "sexual help" video and the husband will be wondering the same thing about his wife…is she thinking of him or "him?"

The other issue with introducing pornography into a marriage is that in many cases, it eventually results in one or both partners going outside their marriage to fulfill fantasies created from watching pornography together. We must all remember that pornography, as well as all other forms of sexual immorality, is a trick of Satan to snare us and to destroy our marriages. If we're not careful, we'll find ourselves checking out websites such as Ashley Madison or even Craigslist personal ads. Satan is constantly creating pitfalls for us because his entire existence is dedicated to destroying what God has ordained.

I have one last pitfall to mention, and I'm sure a lot of you will cringe on this one because a lot of us do this. We must be careful of the television shows and movies we watch…we must also be careful of the music videos we watch…the bottom-line is that we must be careful of what we allow into our homes. I don't believe that we, as children of God, should watch movies that include nudity in any form or fashion, movies that promulgate or spread fornication and adulterous situations, videos with scantily clad dancers gyrating around and shaking their rear-ends or bending over provocatively to attract our eyes to various sensual parts of their bodies. We are children of the Most High God and we can't feed our flesh all week and then show up for church on Sunday to have our spirit-man fed. If we do this, we can't blame Satan when he creates opportunities for us to sin, even if just in our hearts. The Bible tells us in James 1:14 (KJV), *"But every man is tempted, when he is drawn away of his own lust, and enticed."* Those things I mentioned above may seem harmless. But if we are absolutely honest with ourselves, we will agree that those images will get in our minds and raise havoc!

I planned to end this chapter with the paragraph above, but the Holy Spirit impressed upon my heart to speak directly to the husbands once more. My brothers in Christ, we are the heads of our homes and we must be the godly examples that God has called and purposed us to be. We must learn to shield our eyes from those things that would defile our eyes, minds and hearts. The Holy Spirit brought this scripture to mind from Job 31; after all, Job was perfect and upright man who feared God and avoided evil…those are God's words, not mine! As husbands who are followers of Christ, surely we can learn from a man whom God used profound words to describe. I want to share a text with you from Job 31:1, 7-12 using the MSG Bible:

> [1] I made a solemn pact with myself never to undress a girl with my eyes. [7] If I've strayed off the straight and narrow, wanted things I had no right to, messed around with sin, [8] Go ahead, then—give my portion to someone who deserves it. [9] If I've let myself be seduced by a woman and conspired to go to bed with her, [10] Fine, my wife has every right to go ahead and sleep with anyone she wants to. [11] For disgusting behavior like that, I'd deserve the worst punishment you could hand out. [12] Adultery is a fire that burns the house down; I wouldn't expect anything I count dear to survive it.

Wow! This is something that we as husbands must do…we must commit to avoid using our eyes to undress a woman who is not our wife! In other words, we must exercise the power of the Holy Spirit in our lives and turn our head…regardless of how good she looks or how shapely she is! Verses 9-12 ought to resonate in our minds, especially verse 12! Yes, adultery not only destroys our marriages; it will burn down our homes!!!

Chapter Ten Questions to Ponder and Discuss

1. What areas of your marriage do you feel that Satan is attacking the most? Why do you think he concentrates on those areas?

2. What steps are you and your spouse actively taking to combat Satan's attempts to destroy your marriage?

3. What steps do you and your spouse take to avoid personal defilement?

4. What steps do you and your spouse take to avoid marital defilement and marital infidelity?

5. If you have faced tempting opportunities to become involved in "swinging," how did you overcome the temptation to engage in the "fun?"

6. What are your honest feelings about the morality of a married couple watching pornography, whether it's hardcore purchased from an adult bookstore or even softcore videos sold as sexual therapy for couples?

7. If you are struggling with where your eyes are roaming, what are you doing to combat this issues, and have you discussed this challenge with your mate?

CHAPTER 11

Guard Your Marriage

*Be VERY careful about having friends of the opposite sex. If you have
a "friend" that you tell things to that you don't tell your spouse, then
you are creating toxic situation. Affairs don't start in the bedroom;
they start with conversations, emails, texts and communication
that lead down a dangerous path. Protect your Marriage!*

— DAVID WILLIS

AS I BEGAN WRITING THIS chapter, I thought how ironic it is that most of
us who are homeowners will guard our homes by having an alarm system installed to protect those things we value. Okay, so you don't have an
alarm system for your home. Then there's probably a ninety-eight percent
chance that you at least have a password on your cell phone and/or your
tablet. So in other words, you are guarding the information on your phone
or tablet. With all of the guarding we do for our electronics, our homes,
our identities, etc., we often neglect to guard our marriages.

Let's be absolutely clear about something; if we don't guard our marriage, then no one else will! Guarding our marriage means that we don't just
care about our marriage, but we have assessed a high-value on our marriage.
If we don't guard our marriage, then we have assessed our marriage to have
little value. There are probably many married couples who would disagree
with that statement; however, I'd venture to say that some of them...perhaps

even many of them, are in "open" marriages. I've read of some Hollywood stars that are rumored to have this type of marriage. These couples have a marriage relationship arrangement where they give each other a certain amount of latitude to date and engage in sexual activities with other people. So, I would expect those couples to disagree with my statement.

However, every believing couple who is striving to honor God in their marriage...the ones who daily endeavor to obey God's commands for marriage and to be a beacon of hope in a world that is darkened by divorce... these are the ones that must absolutely see the truth in my statement. If you are a believing couple and struggling with my statement, then let's look at it from God's perspective. God ordained marriage! In fact, marriage was the very first institution that He put into place. We can see this from the following text found in Genesis 2:18-24 (KJV):

> [18] And the LORD God said, It is not good that the man should be alone; I will make him an help meet for him. [19] And out of the ground the LORD God formed every beast of the field, and every fowl of the air; and brought them unto Adam to see what he would call them: and whatsoever Adam called every living creature, that was the name thereof. [20] And Adam gave names to all cattle, and to the fowl of the air, and to every beast of the field; but for Adam there was not found an help meet for him. [21] And the LORD God caused a deep sleep to fall upon Adam, and he slept: and he took one of his ribs, and closed up the flesh instead thereof; [22] And the rib, which the LORD God had taken from man, made he a woman, and brought her unto the man. [23] And Adam said, This is now bone of my bones, and flesh of my flesh: she shall be called Woman, because she was taken out of Man. [24] Therefore shall a man leave his father and his mother, and shall cleave unto his wife: and they shall be one flesh.

When we consider the importance of guarding or protecting our marriage, we must understand that our marriages are about us honoring God...in other words, to live with our spouse in a biblical marriage that honors God is a part of our *worship!* We must also understand that anything that is a part of our worship to God, is what we are obligated to do to prove what is God's "good, acceptable and perfect will" (Romans 12:2). This doesn't mean that we prove what is God's good, acceptable and perfect will... rather, it means that we come to desire and strive to live out God's will (*not our will*) that is good for us, that is acceptable or well-pleasing to Him as worship, and which is perfect or complete.

When we talk about guarding our marriage, perhaps a better way to see it is for us to *watch over our marriage to protect it.* Why is this important? It's important because Satan is out to destroy our marriages...yes, I know I've said that several times in this book...I'm hoping we will really get the picture that Satan will stop at nothing to destroy our marriages. Let's look at some ways we can protect our marriages.

MAKE YOUR MARRIAGE A PRIVATE CASTLE

One of the first and most important steps we can take to protect our marriage is to view our marriage as a private castle. In the Medieval times, some castles were protected by a moat to keep intruders from getting into the castle. The only way to get into the castle was for someone, who was on the inside of the castle, to lower the castle's drawbridge and let those on the outside enter the castle.

This is a principle that we can apply to our marriages. Let's consider the structure of the castle. First, there were high, solid walls that could not be easily penetrated. The height of the walls was usually sufficient to keep someone from easily scaling the castle's walls. We must build solid, high walls around our marriages to keep unwanted intrusions from occurring. In our marriages, the high walls are represented by the husband and wife's commitment to have effective communication in their marriage. You see, when a couple has effective communication, they will be able to not only have a harmonious relationship, they will also be able to effectively and quickly resolve conflicts and restore harmony in the aftermath of conflicts. This type of harmonious and effective communication will result in the couple resolving any issues between themselves—and thus the high walls of their marriage castle remain erect and un-breached!

Another aspect of the castle is the castle's drawbridge. It could only be operated from inside the castle to allow someone from outside the castle to enter into the castle. In marriage, the drawbridge represents the fact that those inside the castle, the couple, are the only ones that can allow outside persons to enter their marriage. Please hear me...every couple must especially be on guard for those who are constantly trying to get into your marriage. The "those" include family, whether biological or in-laws, friends, co-workers and even fellow church members. Now, not everyone will mean you harm; but often people with good intentions can cause a mole hill to become a mountain. Sometimes, family members are the worse ones to get advice from when it involves a problem you're having in your marriage. The primary reason is that your family members will often be biased in their advice to you. If you must go outside your marriage to resolve an issue with your spouse, then I recommend you seek a neutral person who is God-fearing and who will provide you with sound, biblically-based counseling.

Then there's the last aspect of the castle and that is the moat that surrounds the castle. The moat acts as a barrier to keep intruders away. In our marriages, we must surround ourselves with whatever protections we need to keep our marriages safe and intact. Each couple must assess the environment in which they live and determine the potential threats to their marriage. We must design a moat or hedge around our marriages. We need to sever previous relationships that can have a negative impact on our marriages...you know...ex-boyfriends and ex-girlfriends...or the neo-relationships out there now that are called "friends with benefits." We can't hold on to those racy photos from previous relationships. We need to get rid of those provocative cards, letters, text messages, the black book, Facebook posts, etc. In other words, sever any relationship that is a threat to your marriage...period! Holding on to these things will breed distrust into your marriage, and offer Satan things to tempt you with. There's a scripture that came to my mind that I believe wonderfully addresses this matter. The Bible tells us in Galatians 6:7 (ESV), "*Do not be deceived: God is not mocked, for whatever one sows, that will he also reap.*"

This scripture is very clear. We will reap what we sow! If we want our marriage to be pleasing to God...to be built on mutual love and trust, then we must plant the right seeds. We must be willing to do whatever it takes to have a godly marriage. We must do what honors God.

When it comes to guarding our marriages, there is one particular issue that has continued to echo from couples who are experiencing problems that include trust and communication issues. The common theme was that one or both were concerned that he or she would change to the point that he or she would no longer be himself or herself. Well, the truth of the matter is that neither the husband nor the wife can remain the same person he or she was before they got married. Marriage is about the *joining* of two persons who become one flesh...Paul called this the mystery of marriage (Ephesians 5:31-32).

We can see this principle of joining if we look at how different metals are joined or melted together to form a new metal. For example, I found out that the metals used in dental crowns include a gold alloy and other metal alloys such palladium, nickel or chromium. When these metals are melted together, they form the metal used for gold dental crowns. In the process of being joined together, these individual metal alloys lose their individual properties and take on the properties of the new metal alloy used for gold crowns. But there is an interesting thing I found out about this process of melting these metal alloys together; it has to do with the great benefits that result from the joining of these metals. Here it is! The properties of the new metal for the gold crown actually minimizes the wear and tear on the teeth that contact the gold crown! Likewise, it is the same for us in our marriages. If we truly work to become one flesh and worry less about losing ourselves to the marriage, then we will have much less friction in or wear and tear on our marriages.

We must be intentional about guarding our marriages. Protecting our marriages cannot be some afterthought or an ad hoc activity. Instead, we must be proactive about protecting the sanctity of our marriages! We cannot have a loosey-goosey attitude about our marriages and about whether our marriage will last. Just as we read in Daniel 1:8 that Daniel *"resolved in his heart not to defile himself,"* we must resolve from the beginning that we will protect our marriages from whatever comes our way.

This reminds me of a couple I know who have been having difficulty in their marriage; I'll call them Tarzan and Jane. In fact, I have personally observed that the husband seems to have little affection for his wife. Perhaps even more so, he seems to treat her with indifference. And it is clearly evident to anyone who is aware of their situation that this wife is starving for affection and attention from "her husband." I recall attending a social event and this couple was also there. I noticed the wife engaged in a flirting conversation with another guy. She was smiling widely and laughing shamelessly with this guy. She was touching him in an almost intimate way...certainly one that showed familiarity. And much to my chagrin, I saw her husband walk by and he practically ignored her...he ignored them! Now, I don't know too many husbands who would have just "walked on by" as if he could care less. Perhaps that was just it; that husband simply didn't care! His attitude seemed to communicate something like, "have at it dude; at least I don't have to keep her entertained!" This probably went unnoticed by almost everyone else at that event. This flirting exchange by the wife and the husband's evidently uncaring attitude is a very, very strong indication that this couple has dropped their guard on their marriage!

I will close this chapter by sharing with you the picture that the Holy Spirit placed in my heart regarding divorce. As I was thinking about how Satan has intensified his attack on marriages in the Church, I was struck by how easy it has become for believers to give up on their marriages and get divorced because of *"irreconcilable differences"*...here's a quick station break...irreconcilable differences is nothing more than a couple allowing their pride to get in the way of them resolving their conflicts...there, I said it...so the next time a brother or sister-in-Christ tell you that they are divorcing because of irreconcilable differences, tell them they need to get over their pride! Okay, back to my story. Satan continues to attack marriages in the body of Christ and we are forgetting what Jesus said in Mark 10:9 (ESV), *"What therefore God has joined together, let not man separate."*

When a couple gets divorced, it is not simply like letting go someone's hand. Look at the verse above..."what God has joined together"... the couple's joining together constitutes them becoming one flesh. When a divorce happens, it therefore becomes a ripping or tearing or cutting of the "one flesh" that has made them one. Consider this! Divorce is like Siamese twins who are joined at the side and who share one or two vital organs as well as life-sustaining blood vessels that carry blood to both of them. To separate these twins is a very critical, major, life-threatening and life-altering surgery. One or both of the twins runs the risk of dying! In this same manner, that's why divorce is so devastating! Divorcees often become depressed...some resort to alcoholism, drug abuse, and sexual promiscuity...and for others, suicide seems to be their only way out of the pain!

As married couples who are believers, we must understand what God meant by Him both joining us together, and His command to let no man tear us a part. That's why we must guard our marriages from every threat, regardless of how small it may seem! I implore you to take no chances... don't allow anything to threaten your marriage! Believe me; if something or someone is a threat to your marriage, then it nor they are of God!

I hope that each of you will take time to sit down with your spouse and discuss whether he or she has noticed any or think there are any potential threats to your marriage. Ensure you develop a plan to fortify your marriage against anything you or your spouse perceives as a threat to your marriage...regardless of how minor the threat may seem! Finally, be prayerful and vigilant as you guard your marriage!

Chapter Eleven Questions to Ponder and Discuss

1. How important is it to you to guard your marriage, and for what purpose are you guarding it?

2. What kind of walls have you tried to build around your marriage to keep others out? Do you consider your walls to be strong enough, why or why not?

3. What issues have you and your mate experienced from outsiders trying to get into your marriage? How did you successfully keep them out?

4. What barriers (moat) have you had to erect around your marriage to keep your marriage safe and intact?

5. In what ways have you and your spouse worked to truly become one in marriage?

6. When you think back to the Tarzan and Jane story, how would you react to this situation if you saw your spouse behaving inappropriately with a person of the opposite sex?

7.   Based on the question above, would you place all the blame on your spouse or would you examine yourself in the process? Why or why not?

8.   What threats have you and your spouse discussed in regards to your marriage?

CHAPTER 12

Never Let Go That Hand

*God intends and expects marriage to be a lifetime commitment
between a man and a woman, based on the principles of biblical
love. The relationship between Jesus Christ and His church
is the supreme example of the committed love that a husband
and wife are to follow in their relationship with each other.*

—JOHN C. BROGER

THE HOLY SPIRIT BROUGHT THIS final chapter to me on January 7, 2015.
I had gone to a doctor's appointment at the Veteran's Affair's Clinic in
Columbus, OH. My wife went with me to my appointment since we
planned to have a lunch date afterward. As we were getting off of the
elevator on our way out of the Clinic, we were holding hands as we normally do. A man who was walking toward us noticed us holding hands. He
stopped in front of us and looking at us with a smile and genuine admiration, he then said something to me that was profound and challenging. He
said, "Hey, don't ever let her hand go! If you do, there will be many others
waiting to hold her hand!" Even though I can't remember his face and I
didn't ask his name, I can't get his words out of my mind...and I don't ever
want to forget his words!

Wow...can this little gesture of holding hands really mean that much
to a husband and wife's relationship? Some of you will immediately say

"Not holding hands is not a big deal!" To you I ask this question; "Are you sure?" I believe that holding hands with your spouse reveals some important things about your relationship. Please indulge me for a few minutes here. Perhaps this is more for the couples who have been married for more than a couple of years. Think back to when you first started courting... yes, you can see it clearly in your mind...there you were walking along together...step-in-step...side-by-side...and you were holding hands! Do you remember the feelings that were generated when you were holding the hand of your mate-to-be? Let me see if I can help us take a stroll down memory lane!

Guys, don't you remember having your woman's hand in yours as you walked along and how that generated within you a feeling of you having "arrived"...that feeling of a great accomplishment! Men, we walked along like we had conquered the world...our thoughts were something like..."Hey world, look at me; I have landed the most beautiful woman in the world!" Remember the fierce pride you felt...the fire burning in your eyes as "your woman" walked along with you? You sent silent challenges to other guys to stay away from your woman because they couldn't measure up to you, or take your place. Do you remember when you had exchanged your vows and "your woman" became "your wife"...you walked down the aisle after the minister had said you can now kiss your bride...you held her hand in a symbol of "Baby, it's us against the world!" Remember the pure joy you felt with her hand in yours!

Ladies, I know you can remember the feelings of your man holding your hand. It made you feel alive as he intertwined his fingers with yours...remember that giddy feeling in the pit of your stomach as you asked yourself..."Is he really mine...I've wanted him to be mine; yes, he's my man!" Surely you remember the warmth of love traveling all the way to your face and you were sure that everyone passing by you knew what you were thinking! Remember the security you felt with your man holding your hand...secure from danger...secure in his love! And of course you must remember the very moment when you became his wife and you and he began the walk down the aisle after the minister introduced you to the audience as "Mr. and Mrs." At that moment, no royal queen anywhere had anything on you...for you were surely the queen of this handsome king walking next to you! The palpitations in your chest told you that this had to be a "slice of heaven!"

The late Michael Jackson did a song, which I consider to be one of his greatest of all time. The song is titled, "Remember the Time." The song verbalizes my urgent plea for us to remember the times I described in the two previous paragraphs. The first two stanzas of that song include the following:

Do you remember, When we fell in love
We were young and innocent then
Do you remember how it all began
It just seemed like heaven...

Do you remember, Back in the fall
We'd be together all day long
Do you remember, Us holding hands
In each other's eyes we'd stare...

So, what am I driving at by this phrase, "Never let go that hand?" First of all, there is something intimate, gripping, and engaging about actively holding hands with your mate. It is a very visual symbol of togetherness! Actually, it clearly spells out to all onlookers that you are not *just* together; rather, it shouts to the world that you are *united*! When a married couple is *actively* engaged in holding hands, it acts as a deterrent to those who might be considering making a move on that relationship. When you actively hold your mate's hand, you are literally communicating to your mate the depth of your love for him or her!

Have you noticed that I have repeatedly used the word "actively" when talking about holding hands? The point I want all of us to understand is that holding our spouse's hand must be intentional...that makes it an *active* gesture instead of a passive gesture. Active hand holding says, "I want to be with you...I'm glad I'm with you because no one else will do!" On the other hand, *passive* hand holding may communicate the message, "I'm holding your hand to make you feel better; I really could do without holding your hand. I'm doing this for you."

Are you rolling your eyes right about now? If holding hands were not important to relationships, then why would God talk about holding our hand, especially since the Bible tells us that marriage is an earthly example of God's relationship with the Church? Husbands, we must take the lead in being the one to hold our wife's hand because we are the symbol of Christ in our marriage. Consider the following verses about God holding us with his hand:

Psalm 63:8 (NLT) - I cling to you; your strong right hand holds me securely.

Psalm 139:10 (ESV) – Even there your hand shall lead me, and your right hand shall hold me.

Psalm 16:11 (ESV) – You make known to me the path of life; in your presence there is fullness of joy; at your right hand are pleasures forevermore.

Psalm 73:23 (NLT) – Yet I still belong to you; you hold my right hand.

Psalm 18:35 (MSG) – You protect me with salvation-armor; you hold me up with a firm hand, caress me with your gentle ways.

Husbands, if you use to hold your wife's hand but you're no longer doing that, I dare you to ask her how that makes her feel. But when you ask her that question, ask her to be absolutely honest with her answer; and let her know that you're not looking for her to spare your feelings. But I warn you; be prepared for her brutally honest answer!

Husbands I dare say that to our wife, holding her hand tells her that she is not just the mother of your children...or the one with whom you share living arrangements...or the woman you married what seems like ages ago. Rather, holding her hand will let her know that she is *still* your girl...the one you chose back then and the one you still choose today! It will tell her that she's the one you want to wake up to every morning and one you want to kiss each night when you lay down to sleep. When you hold her hand, it will tell her that even though time can change the way she looks, nothing can change the way you see her...or the love you have for her!

Your holding your wife's hand will remind her of wonderful times you spent traveling together...of picnics in the park or in the backyard...of quiet, intimate walks on the beach or sitting at a lake admiring the view, but most of all, just enjoying each other's company. Holding her hand will tell her how much you appreciate her, regardless of whether you have been together for six years or 60 years.

I came across an online article, courtesy of Reuters News that really blessed be and warmed my heart about never letting go the hand:

Floyd and Violet Hartwig were married in August 1947. They raised three children; they had four grandchildren and 10 great-grandchildren. This couple was very loving, very devoted to each other and had a lot of respect for each other. In February 2015, both Floyd who was 90 years old and Violet who was 89 years old had both been battling illnesses. As they became gravely ill, they were placed in hospice for two days, but then returned to their home to face the end together. On February 11th after 67 years of marriage, Floyd and Violet both died just hours apart. Floyd, holding on to Violet's had, died first. Violet went peacefully just a few hours later.

www.reuters.com/article/2015/02/26/us-usa-california-couple-idUSKBN0LU2LT20150226

Floyd epitomized the very essence of this chapter; he never let Violet's hand go...he held her hand until his very last breath...until only death separated them. Violet died knowing that her husband held her hand until his last breath!

As I begin the conclusion of this book, let me reiterate that we must be intentional about never letting go our mate's hand until we have breathed our last breath. This requires us to be proactive in maintaining a harmonious marital relationship. Just how can we do this? We must be consistent with performing preventive maintenance and restorative maintenance on our marriage. In other words, we must do all we can to prevent marital conflict. However, when marital conflicts do arise, and inevitably they will, we must actively and quickly work to resolve the conflict and restore the harmony of the marriage.

Just as we must daily crucify our flesh in our walk with God, we must daily crucify our pride in our marriage relationship. We must be obedient to God's commands for marriage and follow them to the *nth* degree. One of the things that have helped our vehicles to last for a long time is that I take them in for their scheduled maintenance. I follow the owner's manual for the recommended oil changes, timing belt changes, chassis lubrication, radiator flushes, transmission fluid changes and service, brake and alignment checks, etc. The reason I do this is because I don't want my car to develop major mechanical problems and strand me somewhere...and because I want it to operate as smooth as possible.

So, if I do all of this for our vehicles, then shouldn't I pay even more attention to my marriage and do preventive maintenance? I've come to realize that you get out of your marriage exactly what you put into it! If you don't do the proper maintenance on your marriage, then your marriage is likely to suffer from a "blown gasket" or "seize up" on you, just like a car's engine that has no oil in it! Therefore, we must do all that we can to ensure that our marriage runs like a well-oiled, well maintained engine!

I came across another online article, courtesy of the Indy Star Newspaper, that is perhaps one of the best analogies that speak to how we can maintain the harmony in our marriages and never let go that hand. In

1966, Irv Gordon bought his brand new 1966 Volvo P1800 for $4,150. On September 17, 2013, Irv passed the 3-million mile mark on his 1966 Volvo P1800. Most notably, Irv's P1800 still has the original engine. The following is an excerpt from that article:

In 1998, with 1.69 million miles, Gordon made the Guinness Book of World Records for most miles driven by a single owner of a noncommercial vehicle. Two million miles rolled up during 2002. Through all of those miles, Gordon experienced very little trouble. "I've never had a scary experience; the car always did what I wanted it to do," Gordon said. "I've driven through ice, snow, took it to the mountains skiing. It's Swedish, loves snow." It was hit a number of times, usually in parking lots.

Common-sense maintenance Gordon swears by regular oil changes, car washes, and genuine Volvo parts. "Just follow the owner's manual," he said. "It's a piece of machinery and can't take care of itself. Have its scheduled maintenance completed. ... Do what the manual calls for, not what the dealer calls for. People who built the car wrote the manual."

He shared a few other tips with Volvo. Use factory equipment parts and one brand of oil for consistency. Spend a few minutes a week checking fluid levels, belts and hoses. "Use gasoline from a high-volume station to keep crud out of your engine," he advises. "It's also good to wash your car regularly and wax at least twice a year." Perhaps the most important tip: "When your car makes a funny noise, listen to it." And develop a good relationship with your mechanic.

Picture this...Irv has now put more than 3-million miles on his car! Getting a million miles out of an automobile engine was previously an unimaginable feat. But Irv not only reached a million miles in his P1800, he's surpassed that mark by more than 2-million miles; and his P1800 is still on the road! There are three pieces of advice Irv gave us about his car which I believe translate to advice that is especially beneficial to us for our marriages.

First, he said to *"Just follow the owner's manual...Do what the manual calls for, not what the dealer calls for. People who built the car wrote the manual."* That's great advice for us in our marriages. We must follow the manual of the One who designed marriage. God designed and instituted marriage. We have already discussed His design and plan for marriage. If we follow His manual for marriage, then our marriages will surpass milestones we perhaps never thought possible. In fact, if we follow God's plan for marriage, we should expect our marriages to last until only death separates us from our spouse.

Second, Irv said to *"Spend a few minutes a week checking fluid levels, belts and hoses. Use gasoline from a high-volume station to keep crud out of your engine...It's also good to wash your car regularly and wax at least twice a year."* Irv performed preventive maintenance each week on his car. He looked for areas of wear and tear. Are we looking for areas of wear and tear in our marriages; if not, we should be! Also, be proactive about looking for areas of stress in our marriages. Knowing what issues are causing the stressors in our marriage will enable us to be proactive about addressing those issues. It could be something as simple as being too busy or trying to be everything for everyone else...noticing stressors like this will allow you to plan for regular quiet time as a couple...to get away for some rest and relaxation...even if just for a weekend or a night! We must be intentional about proactively looking for stressors in our marriage. And getting away for some rest and relaxation as a couple builds your intimacy and puts the wax shine back into your marriage!

Finally, Irv said that *"Perhaps the most important tip: "When your car makes a funny noise, listen to it."* I believe this is also the most important thing for us in building longevity in our marriages. We make funny noises in our marriages...sometimes those funny noises are actually audible... we snort...we hiss...we yell! Sometimes the funny noises are silent, but very visible in the looks on our faces...the scrunched up mouths...the rolling of our eyes...the crossed arms...the closed demeanor shouts volumes!

Husbands and wives, don't ignore any of these noises, whether audible or visual only. These noises are telling us that there is an issue that needs to be dealt with immediately.

Interesting enough, in today's newer cars, we have an engine light indicator that tells us that our engine needs to be checked out or serviced. Have you ever known anyone who continues to drive their car for months without having the cause of the engine light checked out? I have, and their excuse is that "the car still seems to be running fine." If we do this in our marriage, we are not taking care to prevent problems from developing and eventually boiling over...we're not holding our spouse's hand...or for sure, we are not actively holding his or her hand!

By never letting go of our spouse's hand, it means that we have chosen to honor God and to honor His plan for marriage. It means that we are committed to obeying God's commands for marriage and obeying them without prerequisites, regardless of whether or not our spouse obeys His commands. It means that we have chosen to worship God in our marriage and to worship Him in spirit and in truth in our marriages. It means that we are sincere and intentional about the way we love and treat our spouse, and the way we appreciate our spouse as God's gift to us.

By never letting go our spouse's hand, it means that we are committed to avoiding Satan's pitfalls at every turn and no matter the cost. It means that we are committed to guarding our marriage from anything that can be a hindrance or barrier to harmony in our marriage, and from anyone who may have improper or wicked intentions toward our marriage. By never letting go our spouse's hand, we're telling God how grateful we are that He designed our spouse just for us, even with his or her imperfections. So, commit to never let go the hand of the one God gave to you as His second most wonderful gift you. We must resolve in our hearts that we will never let go of our spouse's hand, literally, emotionally or spiritually!

This last story is a fitting end to this book and its theme of "Until death do us part." This story is especially important because like it or not, statistics from studies have concluded that the rate of divorce in the

Church is as high or almost as high as the rates of divorce among couples who are non-believers. As an African-American myself, this story was also important because studies have shown that the rate of divorce for African-American couples is almost seventy-percent, which is much higher than for other ethnicities. But regardless of your ethnicity, I know this story will surely inspire you!

Herbert and Zelmyra Fisher were married on May 13, 1924. In 2008, they broke The Guinness World Record for the longest marriage and became the new record holders for the longest marriage at 84 years. Sadly, in 2011, Herbert passed away at 105. A short two years later in 2013, Zelmyra passed away also at the age of 105. At the time of Herbert's passing, Herbert and Zelmyra had been married for 87 years. In 2010 before Herbert's death, they were interviewed about their secrets to everlasting love and their answers are astoundingly simple! Pay close attention to their answers to the interviewer's questions below; you'll find that we have discussed some of them in this book.

1. What made you realize that you could spend the rest of your lives together? Were you scared at all?

    With each day that passed, our relationship was more solid and secure. Divorce was NEVER an option, or even a thought.

2. How did you know your spouse was the right one for you?

    We grew up together and were best friends before we married. A friend is for life; our marriage has lasted a lifetime.

3. Is there anything you would do differently after more than 80 years of marriage?

    We wouldn't change a thing. There's no secret to our marriage, we just did what was needed for each other and our family.

4. What is your advice to someone who is trying to keep the faith that Mr. Right is really out there?

   Zelmyra: Mine was just around the corner! He is never too far away, so keep the faith – when you meet him, you'll know.

5. What was the best piece of marriage advice you ever received?

   Respect, support, and communicate with each other. Be faithful, honest, and true. Love each other with ALL of your heart.

6. What are the most important attributes of a good spouse?

   Zelmyra: A hard worker and a good provider. The 1920s were hard, but Herbert wanted and provided the best for us. I married a good man!

7. What is your best Valentine's Day memory?

   Zelmyra: I cook dinner every day. Herbert left work early and surprised me; he cooked dinner for me! He is a VERY good cook!

   Herbert: I said that I was going to cook dinner for her and [that] she could relax. The look on her face and clean plate made my day!

8. You got married very young – how did you both manage to grow as individuals yet not grow apart as a couple?

   Everyone who plants a seed and harvests the crop celebrates together. We are individuals, but accomplish more together.

9. What is your fondest memory of your 85-year marriage?

   Our legacy: 5 children, 10 grandchildren, 9 great-grandchildren, and 1 great-great grandchild.

10. Does communicating get easier with time? How do you keep your patience?

    The children are grown, so we talk more now. We can enjoy our time on the porch or our rocking chairs – together.

11. How did you cope when you had to be physically separated for long periods of time?

    Herbert: We were apart for 2 months when Z was hospitalized with our 5th child. It was the most difficult time of my life. Zelmyra's mother helped me with the house and the other children; otherwise I would have lost my mind.

12. At the end of bad relationship day, what is the most important thing to remind yourselves?

    Remember marriage is not a contest, never keep a score. God has put the two of you together on the same team to win.

13. Is fighting important?

    Never physically! Agree that it's okay to disagree, and fight for what really matters. Learn to bend – not break!

14. What's the one thing you have in common that transcends every-thing else?

We are both Christians and believe in God. Marriage is a com-mitment to the Lord. We pray with and for each other every day.

Wow!!!! What a great story of love! I am grateful to God for the example of this late couple. Out of Herbert and Zelmyra's responses to the questions posed to them, perhaps the ones that stand out for me the most are their responses to questions 1, 5, 8, 12, and 14. However, I'll just comment on questions 1 and 14. Husbands and wives of faith, in the words of Herbert and Zelmyra, we must never have *divorce* as an option for our marriage. And lastly, like Herbert and Zelmyra, as Christians who believe in the Lord, we must live out our marriages as a commitment to the Lord…and yes, pray for each other daily!

And now Father, as we conclude this book that has taken us on a jour-ney of discovering in new and deeper ways your plan for marriage, I pray for every individual and couple who have taken the time to read this book. You know my heart and that I am passionate about Your plan for marriage, because Your plan is proven. Father I pray that you will help us to guard our hearts and minds and remain focused on honoring you with our lives, whether married or single. And for those of us who are married, I pray that we will therefore honor and worship You in our marriages, and may You be glorified and magnified, in and through, our marriages. I ask these things in the Most Holy, Wonderful and Matchless Name of Jesus Christ, Our Lord and Savior, Amen!

I close this book with what I consider to be the most wonderful bene-diction found in the Bible from Jude 1:24-25 (KJV):

Now unto him that is able to keep you from falling, and to present *you* faultless before the presence of his glory with exceeding joy; to the only wise God our Saviour, *be* glory and majesty, dominion and power, both now and ever. Amen.

Chapter Twelve Questions to Ponder and Discuss

1. Do you and your spouse routinely hold hands? Why or why not?

2. What things do you and your spouse do that cause you to remember your first love for each other...the moment when you knew everything had changed for you?

3. In thinking of your response to Question 1, how would your spouse describe your hand holding in terms of it being active or passive?

4. What message or revelation did you get from the scriptures of God holding our hand?

5. How important is it to you to have alone time with your spouse, such as going on an intimate vacation or even a long weekend without having others around you that you know?

6. What kind, if any, preventive maintenance steps do you and your spouse take to maintain the harmony and strength of your marriage?

7. In the aftermath of any marital verbal sparring, what steps do you take to restore peace and harmony in your marriage?

8. What are two or three takeaways did you get from Herbert and Zelmyra's story that you want to apply to your marriage?

Contributors

<u>Nikki's Story</u> - LaKeesha N. Leonard, a native of Toledo, OH, articulates her God-given purpose to be *"To give life to the dying, hope to the impoverished, healing to the broken, and to encourage even the more those who are strong so that the royal warrior, which resides deep within every man, woman, and child, will acutely and consistently be made manifest.".* Through the anointing and gift of God she has released two spoken word CD projects titled, "I Speak Over My Life Today...!" (Volumes 1 & 2). Many people have been uplifted and encouraged by these projects and proclaim that they "awaken and activate the spirit man," "break the chains of bondage off of God's people," and cause you to have a "powerful shift in your thinking."

LaKeesha is a faithful member of New Birth Christian Ministries under the leadership of Pastor Kenneth E. Moore Sr. where she serves as a deacon, speaker, and full set percussionist. Recently, LaKeesha stepped away from her career in sports medicine to return to the classroom as a full-time student. Currently she is working on her doctorate degree in Physical Education with a Public Health cognate at The Ohio State University. She is interested in the holistic health of African American women and her primary research focus is on designing a culturally-tailored, faith-based physical activity and nutrition intervention for African American Women.

She resides in Columbus, OH with her loving and supportive husband, Jesse and her endearing and energetic son, Judah.

To purchase copies of "*I Speak Over My Life Today*", please visit www. speakoveryourlife.com.

<u>Phillip and Charity's Story</u> - Phillip and Charity Anderson reside in Louisiana where they faithfully serve under the pastoral leadership of Pastors Nadell and Carol Fullwood. Charity serves as the anointed Praise and Worship leader of Ark of the Covenant Christian Center, a Worship and Word of God focused ministry with a mission to provide "Intensive Care" to lost and broken people. Phillip serves as a minister of the Word of God and youth pastor, as well as an urban missions' musical artist. He has been preaching the Gospel since age 14 and has a life mission to see the world come to know Jesus through the love of and character of His people. Phillip and Charity have been happily married for 8 years. They happen to be our son and daughter-in-law…and they are raising Amaryse, our beautiful three-year-old granddaughter.

RESOURCES

English Standard Version Bible, WORDsearch 10

King James Bible, e-Sword, Version 10.0.5

New International Version Bible, e-Sword, Version 10.0.5

New Living Translation Bible, WORDsearch 10

Strong's Exhaustive Concordance of the Bible, e-Sword, Version 10.0.5

The Bible Knowledge Commentary, An Exposition of the Scriptures by Dallas Seminary Faculty, © 1983, David Cook, Colorado Springs, CO

The Pulpit Commentary: 23 Volume Set, Hendrickson Publishers Marketing LLC, Peabody, MA

Vine's Complete Expository Dictionary of Old and New Testament Words, © 1984, 1996, Thomas Nelson, Inc., Nashville, TN

WORDsearch 10